Food Safety Law and Practice

First Edition

Jeremy Stranks MSc, FCIEH, FIOSH, RSP

Managing Consultant, Safety & Hygiene Consultants, Coventry

and

Wendy Bernstein

Solicitor, Paisner & Co

LAW & TAX

© Pearson Professional Limited 1996

ISBN 075200 1027

Published by
FT Law & Tax
21–27 Lamb's Conduit Street, London WC1N 3NJ

A Division of Pearson Professional Limited

Associated Offices:
Australia, Belgium, Canada, Hong Kong,
India, Japan, Luxembourg,
Singapore, Spain, USA

A CIP catalogue record for this book is available from the British Library

Printed in Great Britain by Biddles

Food Safety Law and Practice

Contents

Foreword

Food Safety is a high profile matter attracting a great deal of media attention. The law which seeks to promote food safety is necessarily complex. This book gives a very clear and comprehensive explanation of the relevant law and, equally importantly, gives practical guidance on many aspects of food safety law including enforcement and the areas of advice which food businesses may seek.

It is often the case that a food business will instruct the same local lawyer who acts in its non-contentious matters. The lawyer may therefore be unfamiliar with food safety legislation which is underpinned by criminal sanctions. This book sets out in a very accessible manner the points which may arise when the relevant authorities seek to enforce food safety legislation. I can recommend this book not only to lawyers, who may be defending food businesses from prosecutions, or following service of prohibition or improvement notices, but also to local authority lawyers and those in industry responsible for food safety. In particular, there will be far less misconceived prosecutions if those responsible in local government for enforcing food safety legislation took into account the possible defences available as set out in Chapter 5. Jeremy Stranks and Wendy Bernstein are both experienced food law specialists. Their work is an indispensable guide for anyone involved in this area of law.

This book has been published at a highly appropriate time enabling the authors to explain the newly made Food Safety (General Food Hygiene) Regulations 1995 which contain very detailed provisions applicable to all food businesses. There will always be cases where a prosecution is considered reasonable by an enforcement authority notwithstanding 'the current cultural shift among enforcement bodies towards clearer guidance, more dialogue, and wider co-operation and advice, in order to support business and improve compliance' (Department of Trading and Industry *Good Enforcement*). Whatever form of enforcement is being resorted to, lawyers, managers of food businesses and enforcement officers will undoubtedly derive valuable assistance from this book both as to the substantive law and the relevant practice and procedure.

Frederick Philpott

Gough Square Chambers
6–7 Gough Square
London, EC4A 3DE

15 May 1996

Preface

Health scares arising from infected eggs and chicken (salmonella) and beef (BSE) have increased publicity about food safety law. More importantly for general practitioners, the growth in consumption of pre-packaged food products and eating outside the home has resulted in an explosion of commercial activity in the food sector. This makes it increasingly likely that general practitioners will need to have a basic understanding of the principal statutory and other material governing food safety law in order to service the needs of food sector clients. No longer can food safety law be regarded as a specialist area of practice.

This book is a general practical guide for practitioners to the key statute governing food safety law – The Food Safety Act 1990 – and two important statutory instruments applicable to most industries which relate to food hygiene – the Food Safety (General Food Hygiene) Regulations 1995 and the Food Safety (Temperature Control) Regulations 1995. The book explains the main food safety offences, considers in detail the defence of due diligence and discusses the administration and enforcement methods relevant to the area. Knowledge of these topics is important for prosecution and defence lawyers alike. For the benefit of the non-specialist, the management techniques commonly used by the food sector to achieve legal compliance are also discussed.

Food safety offences are criminal in nature, most prosecutions taking place in the magistrates' court. Basic procedural issues are outlined in the text which also highlights relevant tactical points for practitioners to consider.

Food Safety Law and Practice is also directed at environmental health officers and trading standard officers, who have the task of enforcing food safety legislation, and managers in the food industry who are responsible for its effective implementation.

The law is stated as at 30 April 1996. Statutory material relevant to particular food industries, for example, the fresh meat and fish industries, are outside the scope of the text. Legal procedure in Scotland is not covered. Scottish lawyers are advised to consult the FSA 1990 and subordinate legislation for particular provisions which may be relevant in Scotland.

We would like to dedicate this book to our respective families – to my wife, Valerie, daughter Fiona and son Simon and to my husband Paul and daughter Rebecca – and to thank Rebecca Youngman of FT Law & Tax for her patience and understanding during the writing of this book.

Jeremy Stranks and Wendy Bernstein
June 1996

Table of Cases

Table of Statutes

Table of Statutory Instruments

Table of European Provisions

Abbreviations

art(s)	article(s)
ASC	assured safe catering
CCP	critical control point
CIEH	Chartered Institute of Environmental Health
DoH	Department of Health
ECJ	European Court of Justice
EHO	environmental health officer
EU	European Union
FSA	Food Safety Act 1990
FSGFHR	Food Safety (General Food Hygiene) Regulations 1995
FSTCR	Food Safety (Temperature Control) Regulations 1995
HACCP	hazard analysis critical control points
LACOTS	Local Authorities Co-ordinating Body on Food and Trading Standards
PHLS	Public Health Laboratory Service
r(r)	rule(s)
reg(s)	regulation(s)
s(s)	section(s)
Sched(s)	Schedule(s)
subs(s)	sub-section(s)

Chapter 1

Introduction

Development of food safety law

Food safety today is regulated by detailed legislation. For centuries, however, the purity of food was controlled voluntarily by traders' guilds. Adulteration of foodstuffs by unscrupulous traders was a particular problem and self-regulation enabled the guilds to protect their members' livelihoods against such practices.

Statutory intervention to prevent adulteration of specific products such as tea, coffee and bread began in the 18th century and the move towards enacting general principles designed to prevent adulteration began in the 19th century. In 1855 a Select Parliamentary Commission was set up to consider the problem of adulterated food which led to the passing of the Adulteration of Food and Drink Act 1860, some of the provisions of which became the precursor of certain elements of modern food legislation. The Adulteration of Food and Drink Act 1860 prohibited adulteration by making it an offence knowingly to sell food containing injurious material. Local authorities appointed public analysts whose services were available to the public (for a fee) and to justices of the peace.

A number of Acts followed in the late 19th century which were consolidated into the Food and Drugs (Adulteration) Act 1928. Food law was again consolidated ten years later by the Food and Drugs Act 1938.

Two offences had primacy in this period: mixing injurious ingredients with food sold or intended to be sold and the selling of food so mixed; and selling to the prejudice of the purchaser, food not of the nature, substance or quality demanded, an offence still on the statute book today. During the Second World War greater emphasis was placed on minimum compositional standards for

1

essential foodstuffs and on the importance of proper labelling of products.

Another consolidation Act followed 15 years after the war, the Food and Drugs Act 1955 which was to remain the governing statute until the passing of the Food Act 1984. Rapid changes in the food sector and food technology could not adequately be dealt with under the Food Act 1984. Instead of overhauling food law generally, the piecemeal legislative approach continued with the passing of the Food and Environment Protection Act 1985 which addressed concerns about contamination of food by pesticides etc. It was under that Act, not the Food Act 1984, that the Government prevented products affected by radioactivity from the Chernobyl disaster entering the food chain.

Consumer concern about food safety mounted during the mid to late 1980's arising from major and notorious health scares. In 1988, Edwina Currie, Junior Minister for Health, said that 'We do warn people now that most of the egg production in this country, sadly, is now infected with salmonella.' This led to a crisis in the egg industry and a wave of regulations designed to eliminate salmonella in chicken flocks. There followed the listeria and bovine spongiform encephalopathy (BSE) scares. The Government responded by a White Paper *Food Safety – Protecting the Consumer* which recommended new legislation.

The Food Safety Act 1990 (the FSA) was passed on 29 June 1990 and came into force on 1 January 1991. In accordance with one of the White Paper's recommendations, the FSA is an enabling act which by s 16 and Sched 1 gives ministers sweeping powers to enact subordinate legislation in response to advances in the food industry and food technology. Section 17 of the FSA gives ministers power to make regulations to implement the United Kingdom's European Community obligations. Although provisions of the FSA have enabled and will continue to enable the UK to implement EU legislation, the FSA itself is not derived from EU law.

Despite the passing of the FSA the incidence of food poisoning appears to be increasing. This trend raises questions about whether the FSA can effectively address fundamental food safety issues. However, it is possible that the rising food poisoning figures merely reflect greater public awareness and enhanced reporting of outbreaks rather than an underlying increase in food poisoning. Another factor may be inadequate resources available to food authorities in order for them properly to enforce the FSA's provisions.

Historically, primary legislation has been supplemented by detailed regulation in relation to specific areas of concern. One such area of vital importance to food safety is controlling hygiene standards in premises in which food is handled and prepared. The Food Hygiene (General) Regulations 1970 (SI 1970 No 1172) (the 1970 Regulations) provided in considerable detail the minimum standards under which food businesses were to operate. These Regulations were amended by the Food Hygiene (Amendment) Regulations 1990 (SI 1990 No 1431) and Food Hygiene (Amendment) Regulations 1991 (SI 1991 No 1343) which were passed to meet advances in the understanding of the interrelationship between the temperature of foodstuffs and the proliferation of pathogenic organisms. The 1970 Regulations, together with the 1990 and 1991 temperature control regulations, have since been repealed, being replaced respectively by the Food Safety (General Food Hygiene) Regulations 1995 (SI 1995 No 1763) and the Food Safety (Temperature Control) Regulations 1995 (SI 1995 No 2200), both of which were passed to implement EU Council Directive 93/43/EEC of 14 June 1993. Food safety standards at the point of production are controlled by specific regulations tailored to the requirements of particular industries, which also in some cases implement EU Council Directives in relation to those industries. Examples are the meat and fish industries. Subordinate legislation also governs the labelling, advertising and composition of food, including the use of additives, colourings, antioxidants and flavourings.

The European dimension

The UK acceded to the European Economic Community on 1 January 1973, following the passing of the European Communities Act 1972.

At the time, the traditional mechanism for harmonisation of Community food law was the setting of compositional standards for foodstuffs, so-called 'recipe' law. That approach was familiar to the UK which had a history of setting compositional standards.

A 1985 communication from the Commission to the Council and to the European Parliament 7674/86 (Com (85) 310) announced that this policy was to be abandoned. Instead the internal market would be harmonised by using the basic principles of mutual recognition of national standards enshrined in Articles 30 and 36 of the Treaty of Rome 1957, coupled with the use of art 100 (issuing directives to approximate national laws which directly affect the market).

Article 30 of the Treaty of Rome prohibits between member states quantitative restrictions on imports and measures having equivalent effect. Article 36 relaxes this rule to permit member states to prohibit or restrict imports, exports and the transit of goods, for example, on the grounds of public policy and the protection of the health and life of humans. However, such prohibitions and restrictions cannot constitute a means of arbitrary discrimination or disguised restriction on trade. This change in policy reflected a trend in the developing case law of the European Court of Justice (ECJ) in relation to the free movement of foodstuffs in the Community. Before the 1985 communication, there had been numerous cases where the national compositional standards of member states to which another member state wished to export its products had been challenged on the ground that those national standards infringed art 30.

The most famous of those cases is the Cassis de Dijon case, *Rewe-Zentral AG v Bundesmonopolverwaltung fur Branntwein* [1979] ECR 649 where the ECJ held that the refusal by the Federal Republic of Germany to grant a licence to a French importer of Cassis de Dijon on the grounds that its alcoholic content was lower than the national standard set for such liqueurs was a breach of art 30.

There are four methods by which the EU implements its policies enshrined in art 189 of the Treaty of Rome:

(1) Directives are 'binding as to the result to be achieved on each Member State to which it is addressed but shall leave to the national authorities, the choice of the forum or methods.' The majority of EU legislation relating to foodstuffs is made by Directives.

(2) Regulations are rules of general application which are binding and are directly applicable to Member States. Regulations are not as prevalent in the food sector as directives. They do regulate certain products such as wine, eggs, milk and fresh produce. Although EU Regulations have direct effect in the UK, a national statute or regulation must be passed to make a failure to comply with the EU Regulation a criminal offence.

(3) Decisions are binding on those to whom they are directed, for example, governments, particular organisations etc. They are rarely used to regulate the food sector.

(4) Recommendations and opinions are not binding, their role is mainly to state EU policy.

Sources of food safety law

As has been seen above, food safety law today is governed by the Food Safety Act 1990 and by regulations either made under it or continued in force by it and by regulations implementing EU food law.

Primary and subordinate legislation are, however, no longer the only sources relevant to the area of food safety. Ministerial powers to pass regulations were supplemented by a concept new to food law, the code of recommended practice, introduced by s 40 (1) of the FSA, and designed to achieve uniformity of enforcement practice. Section 40(2) provides that every food authority 'shall have regard to any relevant provision of any such code'. However, it is only those parts of the codes of practice which appear in bold typeface to which the food authority must have regard. Those parts of codes of practice in ordinary typeface are there for information purposes only.

Eighteen codes of practice have so far been promulgated, a comprehensive list of which appears in Appendix 1. These codes of practice are referred to in the text where applicable.

In addition, art 5 of Council Directive 93/43/EEC places on Member States a duty to encourage the development of industry guides of good hygiene practice. These guides are intended to assist food businesses to comply with the legal requirements governing food hygiene. Regulation 8 of The Food Safety (General Food Hygiene) Regulations 1995 imposes a duty on food authorities to give consideration to whether the proprietor of a food business has complied with any relevant industry guide to good hygiene practice which has been given government approval and has been lodged with the Commission under Article 5(5) of the Council Directive 93/43/EEC.

So far, only one industry guide has been adopted, the *Guide to Compliance with the Food Safety (General Food Hygiene) Regulations 1995*, issued by the Joint Hospitality Industry Congress, through the Department of Health.

Chapter 2

Scope of the Food Safety
Act 1990

To what does it apply?

A non-exhaustive definition of food is given in section 1(1) of the
FSA. 'Food' includes: drink; articles and substances of no
nutritional value which are used for human consumption; chewing
gum and other products of a like nature and use and articles and
substances used as ingredients in the preparation of food or
anything falling within s 1(1).

Food does not include live animals or birds, or live fish which
are not used for human consumption while they are alive; fodder
or feeding stuffs for animals, birds or fish; controlled drugs within
the meaning of the Misuse of Drugs Act 1971; or medicines
licensed under the Medicines Act 1968, except for those exempted
by Ministerial order. Absent from the list of exclusions is water,
which was previously exempted from food legislation.

Since the statutory definition of food is not exhaustive, there
is a residual discretion for courts to consider, as they would
in respect of any other statute, the ordinary and natural meaning
of food. Various dictionary definitions include 'whatever is eaten
by animals or absorbed by plants as nutriment; something
that sustains, nourishes, and augments' (*Nuttall's Standard Dictionary of the English Language*), and 'what one takes into the system to maintain life and growth and to supply waste, aliment,
nourishment, victuals . . .' (*Shorter Oxford English Dictionary*).
Since in relation to food 'preparation' includes 'manufacture and
any form of processing or treatment' (s 53(1)), and the fact that the
FSA covers substances not ingested, eg chewing gum (s 1(1)(c)) and
substances which are not nourishing, eg additives (s 1(1)(b) and
(d)), in practice the FSA is likely to cover everything taken in by
mouth.

There may be a substance which of itself falls outside the ambit of s 1 but because of the circumstances in which it is eaten, imposes criminal liability on the accused. In *Meah v Roberts; Lansley v Roberts* [1978] 1 All ER 97, [1977] 1 WLR 1187, DC a customer went into a restaurant and requested two glasses of lemonade for his children. As a result of an error, they were served with a solution of caustic soda. The cause of this error was attributed to a third party, a brewery employee, who had used the bottle for storing caustic soda solution whilst cleaning the beer supply equipment at the restaurant. He had written the word 'cleaner' on the bottle in small letters and had informed a nearby waiter, but not the manager of the restaurant. It was held that there had been a sale of food for the purposes of the Food and Drugs Act 1955 which, first, was not of the substance demanded and, secondly, was unfit for human consumption.

The FSA also covers food sources which are defined as 'any growing crop or live animal, bird or fish from which food is intended to be derived' (whether by harvesting, slaughtering, milking, collecting eggs or otherwise) (s 1(3)). Where food is derived from a food source for the purposes of sale it falls within the definition of 'commercial operation' in s 1(3) the effect of which is that, although live animals, birds and fish are excluded from the definition of food they become food as soon as they are slaughtered or caught for the purposes of sale in a commercial operation.

Food may be contaminated by substances with which it comes into contact. Section 16(2) of the FSA gives ministers power to regulate contact materials which are intended to come into contact with food intended for human consumption. Contact material means any article or substance which is intended to come into contact with food (s 1(3)).

Where does it apply?

As the Act applies to 'food premises', it is necessary to consider the definition of both premises and food premises (s 1(3)). Premises 'includes any place, any vehicle, stall or movable structure and, for such purposes as may be specified in an order made by the Ministers, any ship or aircraft of a description so specified'. Food premises, on the other hand, means 'any premises used for the purposes of a food business'.

To whom does it apply?

The FSA applies to businesses generally, food businesses and commercial operations, as defined in s 1(3), and to the proprietors of food businesses (s 53). Business 'includes the undertaking of a canteen, club, school, hospital or institution, whether carried on for profit or not, and any undertaking or activity carried on by a public or local authority'. Food business 'means any business in the course of which commercial operations with respect to food or food sources are carried out'.

Commercial operation 'in relation to any food or contact material, means any of the following, namely:
(a) selling, possessing for sale and offering, exposing or advertising for sale;
(b) consigning, delivering or serving by way of sale;
(c) preparing for sale or presenting, labelling or wrapping for the purpose of sale;
(d) storing or transporting for the purpose of sale;
(e) importing and exporting;
and, in relation to any food source, means deriving food from it for the purpose of sale or for purposes connected with sale'.

Proprietor, in relation to a food business, means the person by whom the business is carried on (s 53).

Prior to the FSA, food law did not apply to Crown premises except for National Health Service hospitals. Section 54(1) reverses the position by making all Crown premises subject to the Act and to regulations and orders made under it, unless the Secretary of State has certified in respect of particular Crown premises that it is not in the interests of national security for enforcement authorities to use their powers of entry under s 32 of the FSA (s 54(4)). Without the power to enter premises, the Act cannot be enforced. Her Majesty the Queen is exempt from the Act in her private capacity (s 54(5)).

Although the FSA binds the Crown, the Crown cannot be prosecuted in the courts. Instead the enforcement authority must apply to the High Court, or in Scotland to the Court of Session, for a declaration that the particular act or omission is unlawful and as such contravenes the Act (s 54(2)). The effect of s 54(3), however, is that Crown servants, can be prosecuted in their own right.

Authorised officers of enforcement authorities must follow the procedures contained in the *Statutory Code of Practice No 13: Enforcement of the Food Safety Act 1990 in relation to Crown*

Premises. This code covers the issue of National Security Certificates, procedures for obtaining entry to Crown premises, the conduct and frequency of inspections, the taking of photographs, enforcement arrangements, the position of individual civil or government servants and the service of statutory notices.

When does it apply?

The ambit of the FSA is extremely wide. The definition of 'commercial operation' in s 1(3) covers the whole food chain, apart from farm production, importing and exporting food, its storage and transportation, its preparation and its sale. The terms 'selling, possessing for sale and offering, exposing or advertising for sale' used in the definition of 'commercial operation' are well known to food law and have been judicially considered.

For there to be a 'sale' there must, under ordinary contractual principles, be an offer which is accepted for money consideration. However, by virtue of s 2(1) of the FSA 'sale' is given an extended meaning by deeming it to occur where food has been supplied, otherwise than by sale, in the course of a business. The FSA further extends the meaning of 'sale' by treating any food as having been exposed for sale by the organisers of any entertainment to which the public is admitted (whether or not they are admitted for money) where it is offered as a prize or reward or given away in connection with any entertainment (s 2(2)(a)); where, for the purpose of advertisement or to further trade or business, it is offered as a prize or reward or given away (s 2(2)(b)) and where it is exposed or deposited in any premises for the purpose of being so offered or given away (s 2(2)(c)). Entertainment includes any social gathering, amusement, exhibition, performance, game, sport or trial of skill.

Disregarding the provisions of s 2, there is authority for the proposition that where food is transferred from one person to another for no money consideration there is a supply, not a sale, of food, provided that the transfer takes place in the course of a business. In *Graff v Evans* (1882) 8 QBD 373 a club purchased alcoholic drinks on behalf of all its members and distributed them to its members. The transaction between individual club members and the club was held to be a supply, as opposed to a sale.

The term 'supply of food otherwise than by sale' was considered in *Swain v Old Kentucky Restaurants Ltd* [1973] 138 JPJ 84 where the Divisional Court overruled the decision of the magistrates that the offence of selling food not of the quality demanded had not been committed where the proprietor of the food business, after complaint by the customer, replaced without charge a rotten potato served with a meal because the potato had not been sold. The Divisional Court relied on s 131(2)(a) of the Food and Drugs Act 1955 which clearly provided that the supply of food in the course of a business should be deemed to be a sale of food.

There must be an intention on the part of the defendant to sell the food in question (*Thompson v Ball* (1948) 92 SJ 272). Here, magistrates acquitted a licensee on the charge of selling adulterated whisky where a weights and measures inspector demanded to be served some whisky, because the licensee kept the whisky bottle on the premises for his own private consumption out of sight (see statutory presumptions below).

As the FSA has such a wide ambit because it is enforceable at so many stages of food production, it is essential to identify the actual stage of manufacture or processing of a particular food to a point where the food as a matter of law may have been offered for sale, exposed for sale or in possession for sale.

Food may be exposed for sale even where the customer cannot see the product. Margarine wrapped in paper was held to be exposed for sale within section 6 of the Margarine Act 1887 (repealed), notwithstanding that it could not be seen by the purchaser (*Wheat v Brown* [1982] 1 QB 418) but where margarine was kept wrapped and unlabelled behind a screen out of sight of customers no offence was committed (*Crane v Lawrence* (1890) 25 QBD 152). Bread visible in a baker's open car was exposed for sale even though he had finished his bread round and the remaining loaves would not be sold, because all of the bread was intended to be sold when the delivery run started (*Keating v Horwood* [1926] 90 JP 141).

Food exposed for sale for one purpose may nevertheless be so exposed for another. Milk in a pan on a counter in a shop was intended only for use in tea but nevertheless it was exposed for sale as milk (*McNair v Terroni* [1915] 1 KB 526).

Whether food is in a person's possession for sale is a question of fact to be determined by giving the term its popular meaning as understood by the business community, rather than a narrow construction (see *Webb v Baker* [1916] 2 KB 753, 80 JP 449; *Towers & Co Ltd v Gray* [1961] 2 QB 351, DC; *City Fur Manufacturing Co Ltd v Fureenbond (Brokers) London Ltd* [1937] 1 All ER 799; *Oliver v Goodger* [1944] 2 All ER 481, DC). We have seen that the Act applies throughout the manufacturing and distribution chain. There is little doubt that where food has been prepared and remains on the premises for delivery to the buyer it is in possession for sale. More difficult is the situation where the manufacture or preparation of the food is incomplete, where the food has not been checked to determine whether it complies with food safety requirements (see s 8 of the FSA) or where the food is known to be faulty in some respect. It would in these circumstances be prudent to keep such food separate and clearly labelled 'not for sale for human consumption' to avoid or minimise the risk of prosecution under s 8 of the FSA for having food in possession for sale for human consumption which did not comply with food safety requirements.

The term 'advertise for sale' should be read in the context of the definition of advertisement in s 53 of the Act, which 'includes any notice, circular, label, wrapper, invoice or other document, and any public announcement made orally or by any means of producing or transmitting light or sound and advertise shall be construed accordingly'. The definition is wide enough to cover virtually every way in which a food business communicates with the public. It is important in relation to the offence in s 8(1)(a) of advertising for sale food which fails to comply with food safety requirements.

Presumptions that food is intended for human consumption

There are four statutory presumptions that food is intended for human consumption (s 3). Section 3(2) provides that any food commonly used for human consumption shall, if sold or offered, exposed or kept for sale, be presumed, until the contrary is proved, to have been sold or, as the case may be, to have been or to be intended for sale for human consumption. Any food commonly used for human consumption (s 3(3)(a)) and any article or substance commonly used in the manufacture of food for human consumption (s 3(3)(b)), which is found on premises used for the preparation, storage or sale of that food, shall be presumed, until the contrary is proved, to be intended for sale, or for manufacturing food for sale, for human consumption. Finally, s 3(4) provides that any article or substance capable of being used in the composition or preparation of any food commonly used for human consumption which is found on premises on which that food is prepared shall, until the contrary is proved, be presumed to be intended for such use.

The burden of proof is on the defendant to prove to the court that food, or articles or substances capable of being used in the composition or preparation of food, such as food additives, kept on the food premises, were not intended for sale or manufacture for human consumption. It would be easier to discharge that burden if the food had been stored in a separate room or area and clearly marked 'not for human consumption'. The standard of proof is not 'beyond reasonable doubt' but merely 'prove' (*Cant v Harley & Sons Ltd* [1938] 2 All ER 768; see also *Hooper v Petrou* [1973] 71 LGR 347, [1973] Crim LR 298).

Chapter 3

Principal Food Safety Offences

When to prosecute

Before the FSA, prosecutors were guided by general principles on when to prosecute for a particular offence. There is no automatic duty to prosecute for food safety offences and the prosecutor should consider the general public interest before deciding whether or not to prosecute (*Smedleys Ltd v Breed* [1974] AC 839). In that case, Viscount Dilhorne specifically made clear that, 'in cases where it is apparent that a prosecution does not serve the general interests of consumers, the justices may think fit, if they find that the Act has been contravened, to grant an absolute discharge'. More specific guidance is now available to prosecutors in *Code of Practice No 2: Legal Matters*, made under s 40 of the FSA.

Paragraph 18 Part C of the Code contains a non-exhaustive list of the factors the prosecutor should consider before deciding whether to prosecute as follows:

(a) the seriousness of the offence;

(b) the previous history of the party concerned;

(c) the likelihood of the defendant being able to establish a due diligence defence;

(d) the availability of any important witnesses and their willingness to co-operate;

(e) the willingness of the party to prevent a recurrence of the problem;

(f) the probable public benefit of a prosecution and the importance of the case, eg whether it might establish legal precedent in other companies or in other geographical areas;

(g) whether other action, such as issuing a formal caution in accordance with *Home Office Circular* 59/1990 (except in

Scotland) or an improvement notice or imposing a prohibition, would be more appropriate or effective;

(h) any explanation offered by the affected company.

Paragraph 18 of the Code is not legally binding on a prosecutor for a number of reasons. It is only those parts of the Code which are in bold typeface to which it is mandatory for the prosecutor to have regard (see section 40(2) of the FSA and the introductory paragraph of the *Code of Practice No 2*). Paragraph 18 of the Code is in ordinary typeface and consequently is included for information purposes only. In addition, the language of the introductory wording of para 18 is partly permissive; the prosecutor '*should* consider a number of factors', which '*may* include' the factors listed above.

Although a failure by the prosecution to have regard to the para 18 factors may not constitute a fundamental failure in the prosecution's case, such failure may be used, in the appropriate circumstances, as a means to prejudice that case.

Commencement of prosecutions

Prosecutions for food offences are invariably commenced by the prosecutor laying an information before a justice of the peace who then issues a summons addressed to the defendant (section 1 of the Magistrates' Courts Act 1980; rule 4 Magistrates' Courts Rules 1981 (SI 1981 No 552)).

The House of Lords held in *R v Dartford Justices ex p Dhesi; R v Manchester Stipendiary Magistrate ex p Hill* and *R v Edmonton Justices, ex p Hughes* [1983] 1 AC 328, HL that an information is 'laid' on the date it is received at the office of the clerk to the justices of the relevant area. The House of Lords did not follow a decision of the Divisional Court, also in 1981, that an information had not been 'laid' where a justice of the peace or the clerk to the justices had not personally considered the information (*R v Gateshead Justices ex p Tesco Stores Ltd* [1981] QB 470).

The form of the summons is prescribed by rule 98 of the Magistrates' Courts Rules 1981. It must be signed by a justice of the peace, must state shortly the matter of the information and where and when the defendant must appear. Where, as is often the case in food prosecutions, a number of informations have been laid against the defendant, a single summons may be issued as long as it states the matter of each information separately.

The date upon which a prosecution commences is the date the information is laid, not the date the summons is served (*Beardsley v Giddings* [1904] 1 KB 847).

Service of the summons

A summons may be served on all persons other than corporations by either delivering it to the defendant or leaving it with some other person at the defendant's last known or usual place of abode or by sending it by post in a letter addressed to the defendant at his usual or last known place of abode (rule 99(1) of the Magistrates' Courts Rules 1981). A summons may be served on a corporation by delivering it at, or sending it by post to, the registered office of the corporation if that office is in the UK, or if it is not, to the place where the corporation trades or conducts its business (rule 99(3) of the Magistrates' Courts Rules 1981).

In the case of either way offences, the majority of food safety offences (see Mode of trial below), the Magistrates' Courts (Advance Information) Rules 1985 (SI 1985 No 601) as amended, provide that the prosecutor must, as soon as practicable after the service of the summons, serve on the defendant a notice explaining the defendant's right to request advance information of the prosecution's case (rules 3 and 4 of the Magistrates' Courts (Advance Information) Rules 1985). The prosecutor must either give the defendant a copy of the those parts of every written statement which he intends to adduce as evidence or a summary of the facts and matters which he intends to adduce (Magistrates' Courts (Advance Information) Rules 1985, r 4(a) and (b)).

Even though it is not compulsory, many prosecutors serve on the defendant at the same time as the summons the Notice of Advance Information and the advance information itself. Written statements invariably are in the form prescribed by the Criminal Justice Act 1967, s 9. Many prosecutors also serve with the summons a Notice to Cite Previous Convictions, although such notice need only be served on the defendant seven days before the hearing in the Magistrates Court (Magistrates' Courts Act 1980, s 104). Spent convictions should, so far as is practicable, be marked as such on the notice (para 5 of *Practice Note* [1975] 2 All ER 1072). All food safety offences eventually will become spent, since the maximum term of imprisonment for trial on indictment is two years and it is only custodial sentences of more than 30 months which never become spent (section 5(1)(b) of the Rehabilitation of

Offenders Act 1974; see table A to section 5 for the period after which convictions become spent and *Home Office Circular* 130/1975).

Mode of trial

The vast majority of food law cases are tried in the Magistrates Court even though as stated above many of them are either way offences which can be tried in either the Magistrates or the Crown Court. Apart from one exception, all the offences created by the FSA are triable either way. The exception is the two offences created by s 33(1) of the FSA, obstructing a person who is enforcing the FSA (s 33(1)(a)) or failing to give to such a person any assistance or information which may reasonably be required (s 33(1)(b)) which are only triable summarily in the Magistrates Court.

Selection of the mode of trial is governed by sections 18–23 of the Magistrates' Courts Act 1980. The identity of the defendant is confirmed and, if the charge has not already been written down, it is written down and read out (s 19(2)(a)). First the prosecutor and then the defendant are then given an opportunity to address the magistrates about which mode of trial each of them considers is more suitable (s 19(2)(b)). The magistrates then decide whether the case should be tried summarily before them or should be tried on indictment in the Crown Court. In reaching their decision, the magistrates must have regard to the nature of the case, the seriousness of the offence, whether their punishment powers are adequate to deal with the offence and any other circumstances which may make the case more suitable for summary trial or trial on indictment (s 19(3)). There is guidance to assist magistrates in this task in *Practice Note (Mode of Trial: Guidelines)* [1990] 1 WLR 1439. The previous convictions of the defendant are irrelevant for this purpose and must not be brought to the attention of the magistrates (*R v Colchester Justices ex p North Essex Building Co Ltd* [1977] 3 All ER 567).

Although the magistrates may decide that summary trial is appropriate, it is for the defendant to make the final decision whether to be tried by them or by a jury in the Crown Court. His right to do so must be explained to him and that, even if he is tried summarily, he may be committed to the Crown Court for sentence under section 38 of the Magistrates' Courts Act 1980 (s 20(2)).

If the defendant elects summary trial the case proceeds before the magistrates. If the defendant does not consent to summary trial (s 20(3)(b)) or if the magistrates consider he should be tried on indictment (s 21), the magistrates commence the procedure for transfer of the case to the Crown Court. The transfer procedure is governed by sections 4–8C of the Magistrates' Courts Act 1980 as substituted by the Criminal Justice and Public Order Act 1994. No Rules have yet been made to supplement these changes.

Appeals

Appeal from the Magistrates Court can be made to the Crown Court or to the High Court.

Appeal to the Crown Court

The defendant may appeal to the Crown Court against either conviction (if he pleaded guilty) or against conviction or sentence (Magistrates' Courts Act 1980, s 108).

Rule 74 of the Magistrates' Courts Rules 1981 and Rules 6–11 of the Crown Court Rules 1982 (SI 1982 No 1109) set out in detail the appeal procedure. Notice of appeal must be given in writing to the clerk to the magistrates (r 7(2)) not later than 21 days after the decision being appealed (r 7(3)), unless application has been made to the Crown Court for an extension of time (r 7(5)). The notice of appeal must state whether the appeal is against conviction or conviction and sentence (r 7(4)). Once the notice of appeal is received by the Crown Court, the appeal is entered and notice is given to the appellant and any party to the appeal of the time and place of the hearing (r 8).

The appeal is heard by a single judge who sits with not less than two and not more than four justices (Supreme Court Act 1981, s 74). No magistrate who originally heard the case may sit on the appeal (Crown Court Rules 1982, r 5). The appeal proceeds by way of a rehearing of the case so the parties are not restricted to the evidence put before the Magistrates Court (*R v Newbury (Inhabitants)* (1791) 4 Term Rep 475; *Paprika Ltd v Board of Trade* [1944] KB 327; *Drover v Rugman* [1951] 1 KB 380; *R v Hall* (1866) LR 1 QB 632; *Sagnata Investments Ltd v Norwich Corporation* [1971] 2 QB 614).

Appeal on a point of law from a decision of the Crown Court is available to any party to the case by way of case stated to the High

Court (Supreme Court Act 1981, s 28(1)) or to the Court of Appeal (Criminal Division) by right, in respect of any question of law and with leave on a question of fact or a mixed question of law and fact or against sentence (s 1, of the Criminal Appeal Act 1968, as amended by Sched 15 of the Criminal Justice Act 1988 and Scheds 4 and 10 of the Criminal Justice and Public Order Act 1994). Appeal from the Divisional Court lies to the House of Lords where the Divisional Court certifies a point of law of general public importance and either the Divisional Court or the House of Lords gives leave to appeal (s 1 of the Administration of Justice Act 1960).

Appeal to the High Court

Any party to the proceedings in the Magistrates Court or person aggrieved by the conviction, determination or order may appeal by way of case stated to the High Court on the ground that the proceedings before the magistrates were wrong in law or in excess of jurisdiction (Magistrates' Courts Act 1980, s 111).

Case stated procedure commences with a written application to the clerk to the magistrates for the magistrates to state a case. The application must state the question of law or jurisdiction in issue, (rule 76 of the Magistrates' Courts Rules 1981). It must be made in writing within 21 days after the magistrates' decision was made (s 111(2)). It is vital to comply with this time limit as it cannot be extended by the High Court (*Michael v Gowland* [1977] 1 WLR 296; *Bristol and West Building Society v Hickmott* (1980) 144 JP 443). If the time limit is missed, there still remains the other avenue of appeal, the Crown Court, which does have the power to extend time for notice of appeal under rule 7(5) of the Crown Court Rules 1981.

Magistrates may refuse to state a case if they are of the opinion that the application is frivolous (s 111(5)). The applicant may appeal against that decision by applying for judicial review to the High Court (s 111(6)) (see *Cow & Gate* [1994] *Food Law Monthly*, 13, 8, 5 for a recent successful judicial review of a stipendiary magistrate's refusal to state a case on this ground).

Applicants must ensure that they enter into a recognisance to prosecute the appeal without delay, submit to the judgment of the High Court and pay any costs awarded by the High Court, as the magistrates are not obliged to state a case until this has been done (Magistrates' Courts Act 1980, s 114).

The clerk to the magistrates draws up a draft case for the magistrates' consideration. The draft case must be sent to the applicant or his solicitor and a copy sent to the respondent or his solicitor within 21 days of the clerk receiving the application for a case stated (rule 77 of the Magistrates' Courts Rules 1981). The applicant and the respondent have a further 21 days after receiving the draft case to make written representations to the magistrates (r 77(2)). After representations are made, the magistrates finalise the case stated which is then signed and sent to the applicant or his solicitor (r 78).

Where either the magistrates take more than the above time limits to carry out their tasks or where the applicant or respondent requests in writing giving reasons for and is granted further time to make representations, the final case stated must be accompanied by a statement explaining the reason for the extension of time (r 79).

The case stated must state the facts found by the magistrates and the question of law or of law and jurisdiction which the Divisional Court is to consider (r 81(1)). Evidence before the magistrates must not be included in the case stated, unless the High Court is being asked whether there was evidence before the magistrates on which it could come to its decision in which case the particular finding of fact which it is claimed cannot be supported by the evidence must be stated (r 81(2) and (3)).

Appeal from the Divisional Court lies to the House of Lords where the Divisional Court certifies a point of law of general public importance and either the Divisional Court or the House of Lords gives leave to appeal (Administration of Justice Act 1960, s 1).

Appeals from the Crown Court

Section 1 of the Criminal Appeal Act 1968 (as amended) provides that a defendant convicted on indictment by the Crown Court may appeal to the Court of Appeal.

Tactical considerations when deciding the venue for an appeal

Sometimes the nature of the appeal will decide venue, for example, where appeal can only be made on a question of law or jurisdiction. Leaving such matters aside, there are a number of practical matters to consider before deciding to which court to appeal.

Financial exposure in the Crown Court is greater as the court has the power to substitute the penalty the magistrates imposed for a penalty it considers appropriate, within the limits set by s 35(2)(a) of the FSA.

Appeals to the Crown Court are likely to be longer because the court rehears the evidence. Consequently, legal costs in the Crown Court may be greater than in the High Court. Counsel will have to be briefed to appear in the Crown Court and in the High Court unless the solicitor who dealt with the case in the Magistrates Court holds a certificate entitling him to act as advocate in those courts. Any expert will require another fee for appearing again to give evidence in the Crown Court. The preparation of new evidence to present to the Crown Court can also add to costs in that forum. There may be more publicity given to an appeal by way of rehearing of the evidence in the Crown Court compared to publicity surrounding an appeal on a point of law to the Divisional Court. Wherever the appeal takes place, it is worthwhile for both appellant and respondent to consider preparing before the case ends a press statement tailored to cover the various possible outcomes of the appeal.

Appeals against enforcement

Prosecution in the criminal courts is not the only mechanism by which food safety law may be enforced. Chapter 8 discusses in detail other methods of enforcement such as issuing improvement notices, prohibition orders and emergency prohibition notices and orders. Appeal against these enforcement methods is governed by ss 37 to 39 of the FSA. Detailed reference to those sections can also be found in Chapter 8.

Penalties

Section 35 of the FSA lists the penalties to be imposed for offences covered by the FSA. A person tried on indictment and convicted can be fined an unlimited amount or imprisoned for no more than two years or both (s 35(2)(a)). A person tried summarily and convicted is liable to a fine not exceeding the 'relevant amount' (s 35(2)(b)) or imprisonment for a term not exceeding six months or both.

The 'relevant amount' means, in the case of offences under ss 7, 8 and 14 of the FSA, £20,000 and for offences under any other section, the statutory maximum, currently £5,000. Whilst the maximum fine for an offence under s 33(1), of obstructing enforcement officers or failing to provide information or assistance reasonably required is £5,000, the maximum term of imprisonment is three months (s 35(1)).

Penalties under the Food Safety (General Food Hygiene) Regulations 1995 differ slightly from those for offences under the FSA (apart from s 7, 8 and 14 offences). On summary conviction for an offence under these regulations, the defendant can be fined no more than the statutory maximum, £5,000. There is no power of imprisonment (reg 6(2)(a)). On conviction on indictment, the defendant is liable to an unlimited fine or imprisonment for a term not exceeding two years, or both.

Formal caution

There is also a procedure known as 'formal caution' used as an alternative to prosecution. The offender admits the offence in return for a formal caution, rather than being prosecuted for the offence. Normally, the procedure is used where the authority considers that the offence is not sufficiently serious for there to be a prosecution. The formal caution can be cited in court in the same way as a conviction and it lies on record for three years. Paragraph 18 of *Code of Practice No 2: Legal Matters* refers to *Home Office Circular 59/1990*. This Circular has been superseded by *Home Office Circular 18/1994 (the Cautioning of Offenders)* dated 15 March 1994. This Circular lays down guidelines for the cautioning of offenders. Paragraph 18 of the Code instructs authorities that one of the matters they should consider before prosecuting is whether a formal caution is appropriate.

The Local Authorities Co-ordinating Body on Food and Trading Standards (LACOTS) has issued guidance to enforcement authorities on the use of formal cautions (CO 11 94 5). After confirmation from the Home Office of the following procedure, LACOTS has endorsed sending two copies of the caution to the offender, with a covering letter offering the procedure as a means of dealing with the alleged offence. The letter should inform the offender of the consequences of acceptance (it is an admission of guilt and can be cited in court in the same way as a conviction) and should seek the offender's consent to the use of the caution. If the offender agrees to the use of the caution, he should be asked to sign both copies of the caution and to return them to the relevant office. On receipt, the two copies should be counter-signed by the Chief Officer or other suitable person; one should be kept by the department and the other served on the offender. The Office of Fair Trading should be notified of the caution by sending to it details of the caution on its proforma designed for that purpose, together with a copy of the offender's written consent to the caution, so that the caution can be entered in its Register of Convictions.

Care should be taken to ensure that the caution is drafted accurately so that is properly reflects the underlying offence. It is recommended that it should follow the format used for summonses and, in particular, it should not be duplicitous, ie, each offence about which the offender is being cautioned should be set out separately in the document (see page 14 above and Chapter 5 page 74).

The formal caution procedure is not a bar to the continued use of so-called 'informal cautions' or warnings.

Types of offences

Part II of the FSA re-enacts with certain important modifications the main criminal provisions of the Food Act 1984. It distinguishes between *food safety* offences (ss 7 and 8) and *consumer protection* offences (ss 14 and 15). Technically, failure to comply with any of the enforcement methods listed in ss 9 to 13 constitutes an offence. These methods of enforcement and the consequent offences for failure to comply are dealt with in Chapter 8.

Every food authority has a duty to enforce ss 7, 8 and 14. That authority could be a district or a county council. Where there may be difficulties in determining which authority should take action for differing offences, reference should be made to the *Code of Practice No 1 – Responsibility for Enforcement of the Food Safety Act 1990* which makes clear that both types of authority may enforce ss 7, 8 and 14 but that responsibilities should be divided in accordance with the recommendations of the Code. Briefly, district councils should investigate and prosecute in respect of contamination by micro-organisms or their toxins, for example, salmonella, listeria or botulism and all cases of mould or foreign matter found in or on food. County Councils routinely should check and analyse food for chemical contamination and improper use of additives and take any necessary proceedings, as well as prosecuting compositional offences, adulteration and misleading claims. The Food Safety (Enforcement Authority) (England and Wales) Order 1990 specifically provides that misleading claims under s 15 must be prosecuted by county councils (reg 2(b)) whereas district councils have sole responsibility for a particular enforcement method under s 12 of the FSA, emergency prohibition orders and notices (reg 2(a)).

Food safety offences

There are two specific offences relating to food safety, namely:
(a) rendering food injurious to health; and
(b) selling food not complying with the food safety requirements;
which are dealt with in ss 7 and 8 respectively.

Section 7 – rendering food injurious to health
It is an offence for any person to render any food injurious to health by (a) adding any article or substance to the food, (b) using any article or substance as an ingredient in the preparation of the food, (c) abstracting any constituent from the food and (d) subjecting the food to any other process or treatment with intent that it be sold for human consumption.

As the section applies to 'any person' and it only requires that person to render the food injurious to health rather than being dependent on sale of the food, it is wide enough to encompass many situations where food is adulterated, from the unscrupulous trader who adulterates a product to the criminal who deliberately adds poison to supermarket food as part of a blackmail attempt.

'Injurious to health' is an important term in food law the meaning of which is assisted by further statutory definition and by judicial interpretation. Section 7(2) of the FSA provides that regard should be had both to the probable effect of that food on the health of a person consuming it and also the probable cumulative effect of food of substantially the same composition on the health of a person consuming it in ordinary quantities. 'Injurious to health' must be construed in the light of the non-exhaustive definition of injury in s 7(3) which includes, in relation to health, any permanent or temporary impairment.

It is not enough for the substance added to the food to be injurious to health; the end product itself must become injurious to health as a result of adding the relevant substance (*Hull v Horsnell* (1904) 92 LT 81). Today, an offence would be committed even if the end product was not of itself injurious because it is sufficient under s 7(1)(b) to use any substance injurious to health as an ingredient in the food.

In recent years there has been publicity about food which is dangerous to a tiny minority group within the community, for example, people who suffer from peanut allergy are at risk of serious injury or death from peanuts used as ingredients in food. Section 7 is not intended to make it a criminal offence to use such substances which, if eaten in ordinary quantities, are harmless to the general community. However, a criminal offence may be committed where the substance may adversely affect the health of a substantial part, rather than a tiny minority, of the community (see *Cullen v McNair* [1908] 72 JP 376, where boracic acid added to cream was harmless to adults but could be injurious to children and sick persons and *Haigh v Aerated Bread Co Ltd* [1916] 1 KB 878).

Food manufacturers are protected from persons who make themselves ill by overeating a particular food because s 7(2) refers to food being consumed in ordinary quantities. What is an ordinary quantity is dependent on the physiology of the individual in question.

It has always been extremely difficult to prove the probable cumulative effect a particular food might have on an individual. Much would depend upon the nature of the harmful substance, its relative toxicity and the current state of medical knowledge in relation to the substance in question.

Section 8 – Selling food not complying with the food safety requirements

Any person who sells, offers, exposes or advertises or has in his possession for sale or of preparation for sale food for human consumption (s 8(1)(a)) or deposits with or consigns to any other person for the purpose of such sale or of preparation for such sale (s 8(1)(b)), any food which fails to comply with the food safety requirements commits an offence. The offence can be committed at any of the stages of manufacture, production, processing or distribution of food as there is no specific requirement for the food actually to be sold. This allows so-called 'in-factory' enforcement rather than enforcement only at the point of sale to the ultimate consumer.

Before the FSA was passed, prosecutors had difficulty prosecuting cases where food had become mouldy, rancid or infested to a small extent as an offence of adulteration because nothing had been added to the food which rendered it injurious to health, nor in some cases was a charge of selling food unfit for human consumption appropriate. These cases were often charged under s 2 of the Food Act 1984, selling food not of the nature, substance or quality demanded to the prejudice of the purchaser.

The introduction in s 8 of the FSA of the concept of 'unwholesomeness', that is, that food can only be sold if it complies with the 'food safety requirements' has resolved these difficulties. A negative definition of 'food safety requirements' is found in the Act. Section 8(2) provides that food fails to comply with food safety requirements if:

(a) it has been rendered injurious to health by means listed in s 7(1) of the Act;

(b) it is unfit for human consumption; or

(c) it is so contaminated (whether by extraneous matter or otherwise) that it would not be reasonable to expect it to be used for human consumption in that state.

Section 8(2)(c) is entirely new to food law and it overcomes the problems of charging offences involving rancid or mouldy food. The phrase 'whether by extraneous matter or otherwise' is so wide that it can cover the majority of contaminated food situations. In relation to the term 'in that state', it is important to appreciate that food may be subjected to processing which renders it wholesome to eat and that the food may not be consumed in the state in which it is inspected. The case of *R v Southampton Justices, ex p Barrow Lane & Ballard Ltd* [1983] unreported is an example of this situation. The Divisional Court accepted that a consignment of dates was not unwholesome under the Imported Food Regulations 1968 (SI 1968 No 97), although it had been contaminated with the excreta of various insects, dead larvae, parts of insect bodies and webbing, because the dates would be processed in order to make brown sauce and in that state would not be unwholesome.

The relative unfitness of food is, in many cases, a question of degree, particularly in the case of food which is in varying stages of decomposition or has been contaminated by mould growth or extraneous material. The fact that a particular type of contamination is not harmful to health does not mean that the food is not unfit for human consumption (see *David Greig Ltd v Goldfinch* (1961) 105 SJ 367, DC, pork pie contaminated with penicillin mould unfit for human consumption). Whether foreign bodies make food unfit for human consumption is a matter of fact (see cases on section 9 of the Food and Drugs Act 1938: selling to the prejudice of the purchaser food not of the nature, substance or quality demanded – *Chibnall's Bakeries v Cope Brown* [1956] Crim LR 263 (loaf of bread containing a dirty used bandage unfit for human consumption); cf *J Miller Ltd v Battersea Borough Council* [1956] 1 QB 43, [1955] 3 All ER 279 (chocolate cream bun containing piece of metal not unfit); followed in *Turner & Son Ltd v Owen* [1956] 1 QB 48 (loaf containing length of string not unfit).) In certain cases, the issue of a certificate by a public analyst that, in his opinion, food is unfit, may be a deciding factor (*Barton v Unigate Dairies Ltd* [1987] 151 JP 113).

In the case of batches, lots or consignments of food of the same class or description failing to meet the food safety requirements, there is a presumption, until the contrary is proved, that all the food in that batch, lot or consignment is unfit for human consumption, the quantity in each case being irrelevant (s 8(3)). This section is of particular significance to authorised officers of food authorities when dealing with large quantities of food which may be suspect at the importing or manufacturing stage.

Relationship between section 8 and the General Product Safety Regulations 1994

During the consultation stage of the General Product Safety Regulations 1994 (SI 1994 No 2328), the food industry was concerned that, instead of prosecuting for failure to comply with the food safety requirement, enforcement authorities would use the provisions of the Regulations which provide that a product must not be placed on the market unless it is safe. In theory, both prosecution methods available to enforcement authorities fall within one of the exemptions under the General Product Safety Regulations 1994, namely, where there are specific EU rules governing their safety.

A 'safe product' is one which under normal or reasonably foreseeable conditions of use does not present any risk or only the minimum risk compatible with the product's use consistent with a high level of protection for the safety and health of consumers, taking into account certain factors such as how the product is labelled and packaged, whether it is used with other products, instructions for use and the categories of consumers at serious risk from it (reg 2(1)). One concern was that, although selling a foodstuff containing an ingredient to which a small percentage of the population was allergic was not a breach of the food safety requirement, it could be a breach of the General Product Safety Regulations 1994 which impose a much higher degree of safety as a result of the definition of 'safe product'. Manufacturers thought that they might have to label products warning of every conceivable hazard from it, however small the risk. Caterers and restaurateurs, who are not under a duty to label their food under the Food Labelling Regulations 1984, might have been faced with onerous labelling duties. The Department of Trade and Industry has now issued guidance notes which make clear that where food satisfies the food safety requirements under the FSA it will also satisfy the requirements of the General Product Safety Regulations 1994. Enforcement action should only be taken under the FSA. As regards labelling about hazards, the guidance does not require warnings about every hazard. Whether a warning is given will depend on many factors including 'the severity of the hazard, the risk of the hazard being realised and the type of consumer likely to be at particular risk'.

In August 1994 LACOTS issued advice to proprietors of food businesses to the effect that the use of nuts or nut products in food should be passed down the food distribution chain so that the ultimate consumer could be told either orally or in writing on the product's label of the presence of nuts.

Implications of section 8
Section 8 of the FSA gives enforcement authorities much flexibility to deal with both simple and complex cases of contamination of food. In many cases, the enforcement officer will insist that food became contaminated because of the way in which it was prepared or handled. He may rely on epidemiological studies to demonstrate a scientific connection between an outbreak of food poisoning and a particular food practice, for example, failing to heat meat adequately, cross-contamination from raw to cooked food or inadequate hygiene practices by food handlers. In many cases, a defendant will need to consult an expert either an independent environmental health consultant or a medical specialist in public health or both in order fully to appreciate the legal significance of evidence presented in s 8 cases. Procuring such evidence can be an expensive exercise. Some of the basic concepts which may be of relevance to cases under s 8 are considered below.

Contamination of food may be of a physical, chemical or biological nature. Physical contamination may arise through contact with hands contaminated with dirt, dust, soil and other items on the skin and under the nails in particular. Certain chemicals, such as those used in cleaning preparations, can contaminate food. Some chemicals may be toxic. Bacteriological soiling and contamination can arise through poor standards of personal hygiene on the part of food handlers. Typical examples include:

(a) failing to wash the hands and scrub the nails after using the toilet, resulting in faecal contamination of the hands (*salmonellae*);

(b) use of a pocket handkerchief to blow the nose (*staphylococci*);

(c) hand to mouth/nose contamination on coughing or sneezing (*staphylococci*);

(d) hand to mouth contamination from smoking, eating and drinking whilst handling open food (*salmonellae*);

(e) handling raw meat, poultry, eggs, semi-cooked food (*salmonellae*);

(f) minor cuts and skin lesions (*staphylococci*);

(g) personal habits, such as nose and ear picking, combing the hair, picking spots (*staphylococci*);

(h) handling waste food or food refuse;

(i) contact with contaminated surfaces, eg blood on floors and preparation surfaces;

(j) transmission from one food to another, eg from raw meat to cooked meat (*salmonellae*).

Contamination of food can arise at any point in the food manufacturing or processing chain, eg from contaminated raw materials, contaminated processing or cooking equipment, through inadequate levels of personal hygiene and at the delivery or service stage.

Whilst physical and chemical sources can be controlled by appropriate management systems, the control of biological contamination is more difficult but, on the other hand, vital. Microbiological contamination is associated with a range of bacteria, viruses and moulds which, under the right conditions, will proliferate. (One of the principal objectives of the Food Safety (Temperature Control) Regulations 1995 is the prevention of bacterial multiplication by controlling the temperature of certain foods to prevent this multiplication taking place.)

Contamination by a range of bacteria is, perhaps, the most common form of microbiological contamination. Such contamination results in varying degrees of food poisoning. Sources of entry of bacteria into food premises include people, who may be carriers of a particular type of food poisoning, various forms of infestation, such as rodents, insects and birds, certain raw foods, the water supply, and various environmental contaminants, for instance, dust. Viruses may be introduced through human carriers or raw foods, such as contaminated meat, and shellfish. Mould spores are commonly found on damp surfaces of structures and equipment, on mouldy food and in the air. The various types of food poisoning micro-organisms are shown in the Table of Food Poisoning Bacteria at the end of this chapter (page 38).

Some bacteria form poisons or toxins, and these are of great importance when considering food poisoning. Organisms of the *clostridium* group will develop only in the absence of oxygen and are spore-bearing. Illness occurs after eating food, particularly meat, grossly contaminated with *clostridia* which have multiplied during long slow cooling and storage of cooked meats, stews, pies and gravy. Many of the spores produced, which occur frequently in raw meat, may survive boiling, stewing, steaming or braising for as long as five hours. After cooking, these spores readily germinate into bacteria which multiply rapidly under favourable conditions, including temperatures up to 50°C.

The toxin *clostridium botulinum* is a highly poisonous substance which affects the nervous system causing often fatal illness. This toxin is sensitive to heat, though in its pure form is destroyed by boiling. However, it is dangerous to rely on boiling for rendering toxic food safe, because the toxin may be protected from heat by protein and other substances present. This toxin is produced in food by actively multiplying micro-organisms. It is lethal in very small doses and gives rise to symptoms quite different from other types of bacterial food poisoning, namely fatigue, headache and dizziness in the initial stages. Subsequent stages include effects on the central nervous system, such as disturbed vision and speech, and death often occurs within eight days.

One of the principal causes of food poisoning is through hand contamination of food. There are many reasons why food can be subjected to this form of contamination but they are largely associated with poor standards of personal hygiene amongst food handlers. These include unsatisfactory practices, such as failing to cover minor cuts and skin lesions, hand to mouth contamination and failing to wash the hands in a variety of situations. Because of the risk of hand contamination of food, there is a case for food handlers wearing some form of disposable hand covering, such as fine latex gloves, during the preparation of high-risk foods, such as salads, meat and egg dishes, meat pies of all types, poultry and various forms of semi-cooked foods.

Food spoilage, on the other hand, is associated with the gradual process of decomposition which takes place in all foods over a period of time, the rate of decomposition varying substantially according to the type of food and the conditions, particularly temperature, under which it is stored. Decomposition takes place in meat following the slaughtering of animals, in vegetables and fruit after picking and in other food products following manufacturing or processing. All foods reach a stage where the degree of decomposition makes them unpalatable and eventually unfit for human consumption.

Spoilage may also arise through contamination caused by chemicals, insects and rodents, oxidation of the product and through accidental physical damage. Microbiological spoilage is, however, more important and is brought about by a complex degradation process in foods. Spoilage organisms will multiply particularly in high-risk food products, such as dairy products, fruit and vegetables, meat, fish and poultry.

Consumer protection

The consumer protection provisions of the FSA are covered by ss 14 and 15.

Section 14 – nature or substance or quality
It is an offence for any person to sell to the purchaser's prejudice any food which is not of the nature or substance or quality demanded by the purchaser (s 14(1)). Sale means sale for human consumption (s 14(2)). Three offences are created by the section and prosecutors must be careful not to charge offences duplicitously (see Duplicity in Chapter 5 (page 74)). Often, the enforcement officer can only obtain evidence by purchasing samples of the suspect food to have them analysed. It is no defence that the officer was not prejudiced because he bought the sample for analysis or examination, rather than for his own consumption (s 14(2)).

These offences have been well established in food law for over 100 years. Principally concerned with preventing the adulteration, contamination and inaccurate description of food, they have, by far, been the principal area for prosecution.

Nature. 'Not of the nature' covers the typical passing off offence, for instance selling cod when haddock had been specifically requested, or sirloin steak in place of rump steak.

Substance. Where a substance may have been contaminated by the addition of an adulterant, for example, antibiotic residues in milk, prosecution would be brought for selling food not of the substance demanded. A foreign body in the food does not result in the commission of an offence where it is harmless (*Edwards v Llaethdy Meirion Ltd* [1957] Crim LR 402 (milk containing sterile milk bottle cap)); cf *Southworth v Whitewell Dairies Ltd* (1958) 122 JP 322 (sliver of glass in milk drunk by a child). Food containing extraneous matter may not be of the substance demanded (*Smedleys Ltd v Breed* [1974] 2 All ER 21, HL (caterpillar in a tin of peas); *Greater Manchester Council v Lockwood Foods Ltd* [1979] Crim LR 593, DC (beetle in can of strawberries)). Both cases consider a statutory defence in s 3 of the Food and Drugs Act 1955, now repealed. The relevant defence today is the due diligence defence under s 21 of the FSA.

Quality. Where an article falls short of its expected quality or does not meet some regulatory standard, then it is not of the quality demanded. This could apply, for instance, in the case of sausages the composition of which is controlled by regulation. 'Quality' means commercial quality of the article sold and not merely its description (*Anness v Grivell* [1915] 3 KB 685; see also *McDonald's Hamburgers Ltd v Windle* [1987] Crim LR 200 (sale of ordinary cola instead of diet cola)). A foreign body in food can render it not of the quality demanded (*Newton v West Vale Creamery Co Ltd* (1956) 120 JP 318, DC (house fly in a pint of milk)).

It is necessary in each case to decide which of the three words, nature, substance or quality is most appropriate for use in an information. The courts have recognised that there is common ground between the terms and in certain cases there is an overwhelming probability that the facts fall between terms, thus giving the prosecutor a discretion on how to charge the offence (*Preston v Greenclose Ltd* [1975] 139 JP Jo 245 (scampi containing white fish charged as not of substance demanded, rather than nature demanded); *Shearer v Rowe* (1985) 149 JP 698 (minced beef and minced steak containing 10 per cent pork and 10 per cent lamb charged as nature, not substance). Held in both cases that the prosecutor had correctly charged the offence).

Where a statutory or formal standard is established, then a food article may be not of the substance if the food falls below that identified standard. In *Tonkin v Victor Value Ltd* [1962] 1 WLR 339, a company was charged with selling 'mock salmon cutlettes' to the prejudice of the purchaser which were not of the substance demanded in that they contained only 33 per cent actual fish. The food analyst gave evidence that a mock salmon cutlette should contain a substantial amount of fish, that it was superior to a fish cake (which by law had to contain not less than 35 per cent fish) and that, though no standard was fixed by law for mock salmon cutlettes, in his view its protein content was deficient. The magistrates dismissed the information. The Divisional Court allowed the prosecutor's appeal, holding that there was sufficient evidence before the magistrates to convict. There were three evidential possibilities: a standard may not be fixed by law but, first, the trade accepted that certain substances should be present in certain fixed proportions, secondly, the trade accepted that the article should contain a fixed minimum percentage of an ingredient and, thirdly, (as was the case here), that whatever the true minimum was, the content of the article fell below it.

If the food does not meet a statutory standard, it will not be of the quality demanded. Where there is no statutory standard, it is for the magistrates to fix the standard for themselves after hearing the evidence (*Roberts v Leeming* (1905) 69 JP 417; *Wilson and M'Phee v Wilson* (1903) 68 JP 175; *Hunt v Richardson* [1916] 2 KB 446; *Preston v Jackson* (1928) 73 SJ 712).

In *Goldup v John Manson Ltd* [1981] 3 All ER 257, a butcher sold two qualities of minced beef, priced at 58p and 74p per pound respectively. A notice in the shop stated that minced beef contained up to 30 per cent fat. An enforcement officer found that the sample of minced beef he purchased contained 33 per cent fat. Three analysts gave evidence at the trial of the results of testing samples of minced beef which showed that generally it contained 25 per cent or less fat. No evidence was given whether the samples were of first or second quality mince. The magistrates acquitted the butcher on the ground that the quality demanded by the purchaser was linked to the price paid so the cheaper priced mince could have been the quality demanded by the purchaser. The Divisional Court upheld the decision of the magistrates, holding that the evidence of an expert witness as to the quality demanded by a purchaser could not be substituted for what the actual purchaser contractually had demanded, to be discovered by the express terms of the contract or by inference from the surrounding circumstances. Furthermore, in view of the terms of the notice in the shop a purchaser who bought the cheaper mince impliedly asked for minced beef containing not more than 30 per cent fat. The extra 3 per cent in the sample was *de minimis*.

In *T W Lawrence & Sons Ltd v Burleigh* [1981] 146 JP 134, an experienced buyer of mince ordered some from a butcher over the telephone. She complained to the local authority about its quality as she considered its fat content was much too high. On analysis, the mince was found to have 30.8 per cent fat. The butcher was convicted of selling mince not of the quality demanded by the purchaser. The Divisional Court upheld the conviction, on the grounds that there was evidence that this particular purchaser had been prejudiced because the mince was not of the quality which she had reasonably expected.

The article supplied must be the article actually demanded (*Sandys v Jackson* (1905) 69 JP 171 (sample of milk demanded, not the milk itself)). What is demanded is a question of fact for the magistrates (*Pashler v Stevenitt* [1876] 41 JP 136).

Whether the purchaser is prejudiced as to the food's nature, substance or quality is a question of fact which depends on what information actually came to the notice of the purchaser at the time of sale and whether it was sufficient to put him on notice that the food was not what he demanded (*Sandys v Small* (1878) 3 QBD 449; *Higgins v Hall* (1886) 51 JP 293; *Otter v Edgley* (1893) 57 JP 457; *Preston v Grant* [1925] 1 KB 177; *Rodbourn v Hudson* [1924] 41 TLR 132; *Gage v Elsey* (1883) 10 QBD 518; *Dawes v Wilkinson* [1907] 1 KB 278; *Pearks, Gunston & Tee Ltd v Houghton* [1902] 1 KB 889; *Hayes v Rule* [1902] 87 LT 133; *Williams v Friend* [1912] 2 KB 471; *Batchelour v Gee* [1914] 3 KB 242). Much will depend on the relative sufficiency and effectiveness of the notice given, either verbally or in writing, perhaps, by means of a label, or both. Much also will depend upon the level of knowledge and understanding of the individual purchaser or, indeed, the average customer.

The statutory defence of giving adequate notice was abolished by the FSA but it may still be difficult for a prosecutor to obtain a conviction where, as a matter of fact, the purchaser is told that what he is getting is not what he asked for.

Prejudice is not 'confined to pecuniary prejudice, or prejudice arising from the consumption of unwholesome food. The prejudice is that which the ordinary customer suffers, viz, that which is suffered by anyone who pays for one thing, and gets another of inferior quality . . .' (*Hoyle v Hitchman* (1879) 4 QBD 233, *per* Lush J).

The burden of proof, in the case of selling food 'to the prejudice of the purchaser', rests with the prosecution. This may entail a consideration of the factors which could be of prejudice to a purchaser, namely those factors which indicate non-compliance with the food safety requirements detailed in s 8(2).

For cases involving contamination of food by, for example, foreign bodies, there is a clear overlap between s 8(2)(c) and s 14. Guidance is given to enforcement authorities as to when to prosecute under ss 8 and 14. Paragraph 18 of the *Code of Practice No 1: Responsibility for Enforcement of the Food Safety Act 1990* recommends that, 'cases involving contamination – whether by micro-organisms and their toxins, chemicals, mould or foreign matter and cases involving the microbiological quality of food' should be prosecuted under ss 7 and 8 wherever possible.

Section 15 – falsely describing or presenting food
The following three offences are created by s 15 which are designed to ensure that the manner in which food is labelled, advertised or presented is not false or misleading:

(1) Labelling food so that it is falsely described or for the label to be likely to mislead the purchaser as to the nature or substance or quality of the food (s 15(1)(a) and (b)). The label does not need to be attached to or printed on the wrapper or container.

(2) Publishing, or being party to the publication of, an advertisement which falsely describes any food or is likely to mislead as to the nature or substance or quality of any food (s 15(2)).

(3) Presenting food in a way which is likely to mislead the customer as to the nature or substance or quality of it (s 15(3)).

Commission of the s 15(1) and (3) offences is not dependent on the sale of the food to the consumer as those subsections cover situations where the food is actually sold or where it is offered or exposed for sale or in the person's possession for the purpose of sale. 'Sale' means sale for human consumption (s 15(5)).

The fact that a label or advertisement contains an accurate statement of the composition of the food does not prevent the court from finding that the label or advertisement did in fact falsely describe the food or mislead the customer (s 15(4)).

Section 15 reinforces requirements of other legislation which prohibits false or misleading descriptions of food through labelling and advertising. Any consideration of an offence under s 15 must take into account existing regulations related to food labelling and certain regulations imposing additional labelling and composition requirements for particular foods, such as, for example, butter substitutes (non-dairy spreads).

A label or advertisement as a whole must not falsely describe the food or be likely to mislead as to its nature, substance or quality. Attention must be paid, therefore, to the label or advertisement in its entirety and not just to a single statement which may of itself be false or misleading.

A statement may be false on the basis of what is omitted even though the actual statement is literally correct (*R v Lord Kylsant* [1932] 1 KB 442). Again, a label taken in its entirety, may be misleading even though each piece of information taken separately may be truthful and correct. In *Van den Bergh & Jergens Ltd v Burleigh* [1987] Lewes Crown Court (unreported, BLFD (B132) cream substitute products, 'Elmlea Single' and 'Elmlea Whipping' were clearly labelled with the words 'the real alternative to cream'. The company argued that these words clearly showed that the product was not cream and that the label could not as a whole be misleading. The Court held that the average customer, not being a food technologist and not having special knowledge of this type of product, would be misled by the label, and the appeal was dismissed on this basis.

The courts have frequently considered the labelling of alcoholic drinks and have been prepared to protect particular regional or national drinks against traders falsely or misleadingly using a well-known description for the drink (see *Sandeman v Gold* [1924] 1 KB 107 (port); *Holmes v Pipers Ltd* [1914] 1 KB 57 (Scotch whisky); *Vine Products Ltd v Mackenzie & Co Ltd* [1969] RPC 1 (sherry), *Erven Warninck BV v J Townend & Sons (Hull) Ltd* [1979] AC 731 (advocaat); *Taittinger v Allbev Ltd* [1994] 4 All ER 75, CA (elderflower champagne).

Whether the use of the word 'natural' to describe a product is false is a question of fact for the magistrates to decide on the evidence presented to them (*Amos v Britvic Ltd* (1984) 149 JP 13, where orange juice was extracted from the oranges in the country of origin and reconstituted by adding water after importation into the UK, the juice being labelled as 'natural orange juice' and 'a blend made with concentrated orange juice').

Traditional descriptions of food are permissible where the food is not actually made of the product as long as the label accurately describes the food, for example, 'pure vegetable lard' also labelled '100 per cent vegetable oils' and chicken breast steak described as 'flaked and formed chicken'.

Interaction with the Food Labelling Regulations 1984

Regulation 6 of the Food Labelling Regulations 1984 (SI 1984 No 1305) require most food sold for human consumption to be labelled with:

(a) the name of the food;

(b) a list of ingredients;

(c) an indication of minimum durability (shelf life) or, in the case of food which, from the microbiological point of view, is highly perishable and in consequence likely after a short period to constitute an immediate danger to human health, a use-by date;

(d) any special storage conditions or conditions of use; and

(e) the name or business name and address or registered office of the manufacturer or packer or of a seller established within the EC;

(f) the place of origin if its omission would be misleading to a marked degree;

(g) instructions for use if their absence would make appropriate use difficult.

Subject to certain exemptions, the shelf life of the food must be indicated by:

(a) the words 'use by' or 'best before' followed by the date up to and including which the food should retain its quality and fitness, if properly stored; and

(b) any storage conditions which need to be observed to ensure the above shelf life, for example, storage under refrigeration.

The requirements specific to labelling depend upon the shelf life of the particular food. The following forms of labelling are permitted.

Expected shelf life	Date marking allowable
Highly perishable and likely to constitute an immediate danger to health	Use by 18 December 1996 (year can be omitted)

3 months or less	Best before 1 January 1997 (year can be omitted)
3 to 18 months	Best before 1 January 1997 or Best before end January 1997
More than 18 months	Best before December 1996 or Best before end of 1996

Appendix 3 shows how the required information might appear on a label.

Certain foods are exempt from the requirements of the regulations, namely: fresh fruit and vegetables which have not been peeled or cut into pieces; wine; alcoholic drinks (10 per cent or more alcoholic strength); soft drinks (greater than 5 litres for catering premises); flour confectionery and bread; vinegar; salt; sugar; chewing gum; and edible ices.

The regulations make it an offence to sell foods bearing an expired use by date and for anyone, other than the person originally responsible for applying the date mark, to change it.

Generally, the regulations do not apply to the hotel and catering industry unless food is actually manufactured or prepared on the premises for consumption off or away from the premises as, for instance, with a take-away facility provided by a restaurant or hotel. In such cases, food must comply with the labelling requirements of the regulations.

Consumer Protection Provisions of the FSA and Trade Descriptions Act

The Trade Descriptions Act 1968 (TDA) places general and specific duties on manufacturers and suppliers of goods to ensure that goods are appropriately and correctly described. Inevitably there will be some overlap between the requirements of the TDA and those of the FSA and regulations with regard to labelling and descriptions applied to food. Generally, matters relating to food should be dealt with under the FSA and subordinate regulations.

Table of Food Poisoning Bacteria

Type of bacteria	Main sources and vehicles	Cause of illness	Symptoms	Incubation period	Duration
Salmonella (Infection)	Human and animal intestine, meat, eggs, poultry	Infection by living bacteria on food	Fever, diarrhoea, vomiting, abdominal pains. Can be fatal in the elderly, very young and the sick	6–72 hours, usually 12–36 hours	1–7 days
Staphylococcus aureus	Nose, throat, cuts and boils, contaminates high risk food	Toxin from growth of bacteria in food	Acute vomiting, pain in abdomen. Sub-normal temperatures, prostration	1–6 hours	6–24 hours
Clostridium perfringens	Meat, gravy, soil, dust, flies	Toxin released in intestine from living bacteria swallowed	Abdominal pain, diarrhoea, rarely vomiting. May be fatal in elderly and sick people	8–22 hours, usually 12–18 hours	12–48 hours
Clostridium botulinum	Soil, meat and fish, preserved, vacuum-packed and canned foods	Toxin from growth of bacteria	Difficulties in swallowing, talking and breathing; double vision and paralysis of cranial nerves. Death is common; recovery takes several months	2 hours–8 days, usually 12–36 hours	Death, 24 hours
Bacillus cereus	(i) Cooked rice (ii) Cereals and cereal-based products, dust and soil	Toxin from growth of bacteria in food	(i) Vomiting types: nausea, vomiting, diarrhoea later on (ii) Diarrhoea types: diarrhoea, abdominal pain, rarely vomiting	1–5 hours / 8–16 hours	12–24 hours / 24–48 hours
Vibrio para-haemolyticus (Infection)	Sea foods and coastal waters	Infection by living bacteria in food	Acute diarrhoea, abdominal pain, vomiting, dehydration	2–48 hours, usually 12–18 hours	1–7 days

continued

Type of bacteria	Main sources and vehicles	Cause of illness	Symptoms	Incubation period	Duration
Escherichia coli (Infection and toxin)	Human and animal intestine, poultry, pet meat	Infection by living bacteria in food	Pain, diarrhoea, sometimes pyrexia and vomiting	10–72 hours, usually 12–24 hours	1–5 days
Food-borne infections					
Campylobacter	Unpasteurised milk, animals and birds, sewage	Infection by living bacteria in food	Moderate to severe diarrhoea, rarely vomiting, severe cramping abdominal pain, pyrexia in early stages, headache	2–5 days	1–7 days
Listeria Monocytogenes	Milk, ice cream, variable cheese, meats, seafoods, prepacked salads, very wide distribution	Very pathogenic infection by living bacteria in food	Septicaemia, fever, abortion; meningitis, particularly in infants, elderly and immuno-suppressed people		

Chapter 4

Food Safety (General Food Hygiene) Regulations 1995 and Food Safety (Temperature Control) Regulations 1995

Introduction

These regulations, which implement the requirements of the European Community Council Directive 93/43/EEC of 14 June 1993 on the hygiene of foodstuffs (the Directive), came into operation on 15 September 1995. They revoke a substantial part of the old food hygiene legislation, in particular the Food Hygiene (General) Regulations 1970, the Food Hygiene (Markets, Stalls and Delivery Vehicles) Regulations 1966 (SI 1966 No 791) and the Food Hygiene (Amendment) Regulations 1990 and 1991. Both regulations should be read in conjunction with the various statutory codes issued under the FSA and Guides to Good Hygiene Practice issued by the Department of Health on these matters.

The Food Safety (General Food Hygiene) Regulations 1995 (SI 1995 No 1763) represent a new departure in the way food hygiene law will operate in the UK. Apart from identifying general obligations (as opposed to 'duties') on proprietors of food businesses, the actual regulations are quite short. The detail is to be found in Schedule 1, Rules of Hygiene, which are taken direct from the Annex to the Directive.

The Food Safety (Temperature Control) Regulations 1995, (SI 1995 No 2200) simplify previous domestic regulations. They remove the list in current regulations of foods subject to chill control, set a single maximum chill temperature of 8°C, removing the former two-tier controls of 5°C and 8°C, allow flexibility for certain food businesses to vary the 8°C maximum upwards, where a well-founded scientific assessment justifies this, and implement the general requirements of the Directive for certain foods to be kept 'at temperatures which would not result in a risk to health' (Chapter IX, para 4 to Annex of the Directive).

Food Safety (General Food Hygiene) Regulations 1995

The Food Safety (General Food Hygiene) Regulations 1995 (FSGFHR) implement the requirements of Council Directive 93/43/EEC of 14 June 1993 on the hygiene of foodstuffs (the Directive), apart from paras 4 and 5 of Chapter IX of the Annex to that Directive (which relate to temperature controls) and for the requirements in that Directive which relate to imports which are likely to pose a serious risk to human health and which come from countries outside the EC. They also implement provisions of Council Directive 80/778/EEC of 15 July 1980 relating to the quality of water intended for human consumption (the Water Quality Directive) which relate to the use of water for food production purposes. The FSGFHR feature a number of general requirements which are amplified in the comprehensive 'Rules of Hygiene' incorporated as a Schedule to them.

Guidance on the FSGFHR

Guidance on the FSGFHR has been issued by the Department of Health (DoH). This Guidance is principally directed at enforcement officers, who need to interpret them.

Industry guides
Article 5 of the Directive places on Member States a duty to encourage the development of industry guides to good hygiene practice. Accordingly, the FSGFHR will be supported by a series of voluntary industry guides prepared and developed by various sectors of the food industry. The aim of these guides is to provide a business sector guide to compliance with legal obligations and practices specific to an industry sector which are generally necessary to secure the safety and wholesomeness of food.

Completed industry guides can be submitted to the DoH for recognition. Where a food business is clearly following advice in a recognised guide, this must be given due consideration by enforcers when assessing compliance with the requirements of the FSGFHR (reg 8(2)(c) of the FSGFHR).

Recognised guides can be used with confidence by food businesses as a practical guide to compliance with the FSGFHR but there is no legal requirement that every member of the food industry must follow the guides. Guides set out recommended means of achieving legislative objectives, but other means may be possible (*Department of Health [1994] EC Food Hygiene Directive: A Template: Industry Guides to Good Hygiene Practice*).

DoH guidance advises that industry guides cannot be used as a standard in any legal proceedings because the FSGFHR are what have to be complied with, not voluntary industry guides, although the courts may accept industry guides as supporting evidence. The guides may be useful to defendants in defending themselves in court. Ultimately, it is the court which must decide to what extent, if any, to take advice in industry guides into account.

General Features of the FSGFHR

To what industries and businesses do the FSGFHR apply?
The FSGFHR do not list the food industry sectors to which they apply. Instead, they exempt from their provisions certain industry sectors. First, primary production which includes harvesting, slaughter and milking (reg 3(1)(a)) is excluded. DoH guidance states that once the action of harvesting vegetables or fruit has been completed, for example when the vegetables are being placed on a trailer for transport out of the field, the regulations will apply. The risk-related nature of many of the provisions of the regulations means, however, that the low risk nature of products such as freshly picked vegetables or fruit must be taken into account in applying some of the individual requirements.

Secondly, those sectors for which there are existing regulations implementing vertical EC Directives relating to specific industry sectors, such as the fish, egg, meat, poultry and dairy industries (reg 3(2)(b)) are excluded. However, the FSGFHR do apply to those industries where existing regulations do not impose further or alternative requirements on the proprietor of the food business in relation to the supply and use of potable water and the training of food handlers (reg 3(3) and (4)). It is clear from the language of reg 4 that all of the following stages of food production are covered by the FSGFHR: preparation, processing, manufacturing, packaging, storing, transportation, distribution, handling and offering to sell or supply food.

The FSGFHR apply where any one of those activities is carried on at the premises of food businesses irrespective of whether those premises are movable or temporary premises (such as market stalls, marquees, mobile sales vehicles), private homes, premises used occasionally for those purposes and vending machines, although the legal requirements imposed in respect of these types of premises are not as demanding (see Chapter III of the Rules of Hygiene, Sched 1 of the FSGFHR).

Like the FSA, the FSGFHR apply to food businesses whether or not they are carried on for profit. Whereas the definition of 'business' in s 1(3) of the FSA refers to 'the undertaking of a canteen, club, school, hospital or institution . . . and any undertaking or activity carried on by a public or local authority', the definition of 'food business' in reg 2(1) of the FSGFHR merely refers to 'any undertaking, whether carried on for profit or not and whether public or private, carrying out any or all of the following operations, namely, preparation, processing, manufacture, packaging, storage, transportation, distribution, handling or offering for sale or supply, of food'. The FSGFHR definition derives from the definition of 'food business' in art 2 of the Directive. The extended meaning of 'sale' given in s 2 of the FSA applies to the FSGFHR (reg 7(a)).

The general food hygiene obligations of proprietors

Operate the business in a hygienic way. The primary obligation of the food business proprietor is to ensure that he carries out his operation in a hygienic way (regulation 4 (1)).

DoH guidance clarifies that 'proprietor' in relation to a food business means the person by whom the business is carried on (s 53 of the FSA). This can be either a manager or owner of a food business depending upon the precise relationship between the person concerned and their level of involvement in the food business.

'Hygiene' is defined in reg 2 as meaning 'all measures necessary to ensure the safety and wholesomeness of food at all stages after primary production, during preparation, processing, manufacture, packaging, storage, transportation, distribution, handling and offering for sale or supply to the consumer, and hygienic shall be construed accordingly'. 'Wholesomeness' is defined in reg 2(1) as meaning 'in relation to food, its fitness for human consumption so far as hygiene is concerned'. These definitions both derive from the Directive (art 2). The presumption that food is intended for human consumption set out in s 3 of the FSA is incorporated into the FSGFHR (reg 7(b)). DoH guidance states that the term 'wholesomeness' is not intended to relate to the nutritional qualities of food but just to whether it is fit for human consumption.

The definition of 'wholesomeness' is amplified by two further definitions in the FSGFHR. Regulation 2(2) provides that, 'in determining whether any matter involves a risk to food safety or wholesomeness, regard shall be had to the nature of the food, the manner in which it is handled and packed, any process to which the food is subjected before supply to the consumer, and the conditions under which it is displayed or stored. Regulation 2(2) is important, implying that all four factors, namely, 'nature', 'manner', 'process' and 'condition', must be considered by the food authority in determining whether a risk to food safety exists. Secondly, the Rules of Hygiene in Schedule 1 to the FSGFHR often refer to something being done, 'where appropriate' or 'where necessary'. Regulation 2(3) provides that these terms 'mean where appropriate and where necessary respectively for the purposes of ensuring the safety and wholesomeness of food'. *Code of Practice No 9: Food Hygiene Inspections* (revised September 1995), paras 78 and 79, instruct enforcement officers that these terms denote that requirements may not be needed to achieve food safety in the particular business. It is likely that the interpretation of these terms will be controversial, both at enforcement level and as a question of fact ultimately to be decided by a court.

Although the concept of 'wholesomeness' of food is incorporated in the definition of 'food safety requirements' in s 8(2) of the FSA, it is important only to use the definitional terms of the FSGFHR in cases related to it. However, it is interesting to note that in imposing an obligation to protect food against the risk of contamination, para 3 of Chapter IX of Sched 1 lists the constituent elements of the definition of 'food safety requirements' in s 8(2), namely, 'render[ing] the food unfit for human consumption, injurious to health or contaminated in such a way that it would be unreasonable to expect it to be consumed in that state'.

Obligation to comply with the Rules of Hygiene. Supplemental to the primary obligation to operate the food business in a hygienic way, is the requirement in reg 4(2) for the proprietor of the food business to ensure compliance with the detailed Rules of Hygiene set out in Sched 1 to the Regulations. Chapters I to III of Sched 1 set out the requirements for food premises, rooms where food is prepared, treated or processed, temporary premises etc. and vending machines. The Rules of Hygiene also cover transportation, requirements as to equipment, food waste, water supply and personal hygiene, provisions applicable to foodstuffs and training (Chapters IV to X respectively).

Obligation to implement hazard analysis critical control points. It is compulsory for the proprietor of a food business to identify steps in the activities of the business which are critical to ensuring food safety and to ensure that adequate safety procedures are identified, implemented, maintained and reviewed (reg 4(3)). This process is known as Hazard Analysis Critical Control Points (HACCP). Accordingly, proprietors of food businesses will have to develop and operate food safety management techniques such as HACCPs and Assured Safe Catering (ASC). This will entail the provision of information, instruction and training, together with the appropriate documentation of the control and monitoring procedures, to ensure compliance. Where enforcement officers find that food safety management techniques are absent or ineffective, DoH guidance states that it may be appropriate for an enforcement officer to issue an improvement notice on hazard analysis requirements, particularly for high risk operations where a more formal type of hazard analysis system is needed.

Food handler's obligation to notify disease to proprietor. Persons working in food handling areas who either know or suspect that they carry a disease likely to be transmitted through food or who have an infected wound, a skin infection, sores, diarrhoea or analogous medical condition from which there is a likelihood of directly or indirectly contaminating food with pathogenic micro-organisms must report their illness or suspicion of illness to the food business proprietor (reg 5(1)). DoH guidance advises that the report should be made to the food handler's manager or supervisor immediately. The food business proprietor is required by para 2 of Chapter VIII of Sched 1 to refuse that person permission to work in the food handling area. Such action should be taken urgently and if there is any doubt about the need to exclude, the business should seek urgent medical advice or consult the local authority Environmental Health Department. Helpful guidance is contained in, *Food Handlers: Fitness to Work*, available by post from the DoH.

The employee can return to work only when he can show that the illness no longer presents a risk. If there is any doubt about the position, then medical advice, or that of the local authority Environmental Health Department, should be sought. The provisions concerning financial compensation have not been altered under the 1995 Regulations. Compensation can be given by the local authority to both food businesses and individual employees at the discretion of the authority, unless specifically directed by the court.

Where a business does not exclude an infected food handler, the business would be committing an offence if there is any likelihood of the person directly or indirectly contaminating food. The local authority Environmental Health Department will also continue to have reserve powers by service of an emergency prohibition notice on the individual or individuals concerned to exclude infected food handlers from the business if the business itself does not act.

Offences created by the FSGFHR. It is an offence under the FSGFHR to contravene any part of reg 4 and any provision of Sched 1, that is, any of the detailed rules of hygiene (reg 6(1)). An example given in the DoH guidance is of dirty premises and a lavatory connecting directly to a preparation room which would be a breach of two different requirements, ie reg 4(2)(a), Sched 1, Chapter I, paras 1 and 3. It would therefore be two offences.

Like the majority of the offences created by the FSA, offences under the FSGFHR are triable either way (see Chapter III: commencement of prosecution). The only penalty on summary conviction is a maximum fine of £5,000; magistrates have no power to imprison offenders under the FSGFHR (reg 6(2)). The penalties on conviction on indictment are the same as in the FSA, an unlimited fine or imprisonment for not more than two years or both. The time limits for prosecuting offences under the FSA are the same as those in s 34 of the FSA (reg 7(g)). Those time limits are discussed in detail in Chapter 5 (pp 72–4).

Where the offence has been committed by the food business proprietor because of the act or default of someone other than him, that other person can be prosecuted by the food authority (reg 7(c), applying s 20 of the FSA). Accordingly, enforcement action could be considered against managers with relevant responsibilities where the proprietor is not responsible for commission of an offence. Chapter 5, pp 78–9, refers to s 20 in detail, as well as offences committed by bodies corporate. The definition of 'bodies corporate', in s 36 of the FSA is incorporated into the FSGFHR with minor modifications referred to in reg 7(h) of the FSGFHR.

Enforcement of the FSGFHR. The responsibility for enforcement of the FSGFHR rests with the food authority of the area in which the relevant offence has been committed. The food authorities of England and Wales are listed in s 5 of the FSA which is discussed in Chapter 6 (p 96). Although under the FSA, county councils for non-metropolitan areas are designated food authorities, they are not responsible for enforcement of the FSGFHR (reg 2(1)). That duty rests only with district councils.

Food authorities have a statutory duty to inspect food premises as regularly as the risks associated with those premises require (reg 8(2)(a)). Statutory guidance is given on what should be considered during such inspections. The enforcement officer should make a general assessment of the food safety hazards associated with the particular business. In so doing, he should consider the critical control points identified by the business during its hazard analysis so that he can assess whether the monitoring and verification controls devised by the business are being operated and, as discussed in the introduction to this chapter, whether the food business has complied with any relevant industry guides (reg 8(2)(a)(ii), (b) and (c)).

Inspection procedures operated by food authorities are subject to a number of statutory codes issued under the FSA, in particular *Code of Practice No 3: Inspection Procedures–General* and *Code of Practice No 9: Food Hygiene Inspections* (revised September 1995). When advising on food hygiene issues, officers must clearly distinguish between legal requirements and good practice (*Code of Practice No 9*, para 51). Inspection procedures entail an element of risk assessment taking into account the critical control points, monitoring arrangements and controls installed, such as cleaning programmes, infestation control procedures and temperature control arrangements. Sections K and L of *Code of Practice No 9* give detailed advice to enforcement officers about enforcing hazard analysis and food hygiene training.

Schedule 1 – rules of hygiene

Schedule 1 to the FSGFHR, which is divided into ten 'chapters', lays down detailed general and specific legal requirements pertaining to the hygienic operation of a food business.

The importance of analysing the terminology used in Schedule 1
Although offences under the FSGFHR are offences of strict liability where the only statutory defence is that of due diligence (reg 7(d) and see Chapter 5), it should always be borne in mind that the burden of proof rests with the prosecution to prove beyond reasonable doubt that the offence charged has been committed. Reaching the standard of proof may involve close scrutiny of the wording of that part of Sched 1 which it is alleged the defendant has infringed.

Interpretation of many of the terms frequently used in Sched 1, such as, 'where necessary', 'where appropriate', 'suitable', 'sufficient', 'reasonably practicable', 'risk of contamination' and 'adequate', will necessarily be subjective. Apart from 'where necessary' and 'where appropriate', none is defined in the FSGFHR (see reg 2(3)). In the context of section 13 of the Food and Drugs Act 1955 which authorised the making of regulations to secure the observance of hygienic practices, *inter alia*, to protect public health, the term 'risk of contamination', used in the Food Hygiene Regulations 1955 made pursuant to s 13 has been held to mean, 'risk of contamination injurious to health' (*MacFisheries (Wholesale & Retail) Ltd v Coventry Corporation* [1957] 3 All ER 299). Section 16 of the FSA, under which the FSGFHR are made, refers to ministers making regulations 'for the purpose of securing that food complies with food safety requirements or in the interests of the public health' (s 16(1)(f)(i)).

The interpretation of all these terms initially rests with the enforcement officer inspecting the food premises and it will be dependent upon the particular factual context in which they arise. For example, what may be 'adequate' in the context of a small catering operation may not be 'adequate' for a manufacturing operation. Enforcement officers should interpret these terms taking into account the nature and size of the undertaking being inspected. Prosecutors should assess whether there is evidence available to support the view reached by the enforcement officer.

When considering available defences to charges made under Sched 1, it is advisable for defence solicitors carefully to analyse the wording of that part of Schedule 1 alleged to have been infringed. Given the appropriate evidence, it may be possible to persuade the court that the prosecution has failed to prove the offence charged. For example, some enforcement authorities insist that sneeze screens should be installed over self-service counters in staff canteens, restaurants etc. A prosecution for failing to have a sneeze screen so as to minimise any risk of contamination of food, contrary to para 3 of Chapter IX of Sched 1, could be challenged if bacteriological evidence is called to demonstrate that there is no risk of contamination to food which is likely to render it injurious to health, unfit for human consumption or which would so contaminate that it would be unreasonable to expect it to be consumed in that state. *The Catering Industry's Guide to Good Hygiene Practice* advises that sneeze screens are not a legal requirement under para 3 of Chapter IX but that, as a matter of good practice, they, 'may play a small part in reducing airborne contamination'.

Where the prosecution relies on an argument that a particular practice is, 'necessary' or 'appropriate' it will have to demonstrate that such practice is necessary or appropriate for ensuring the safety and wholesomeness of the food. This may require evidence of a bacteriological nature, in particular, and of failure to implement basic 'clean place' and 'clean person' strategies in the running of the business.

Clean place strategies are concerned with the structural, environmental and organisational aspects of hygiene control, and include the provision and maintenance of clean premises, clean plant and equipment, clean processes, a clean environment, clean systems of work, adequate supervision and control, and competent and trained staff. The main aim of a 'clean place' strategy is to bring about a reduction in the physical, chemical and biological conditions which may lead to a food hygiene incident.

Clean person strategies are directed at people, in particular food handlers, and include ensuring adequate levels of personal hygiene, the provision and proper use of personal protective equipment, health surveillance, selection and placement of staff, the provision and correct use of welfare amenity provisions, adequate supervision and control, and the employment of competent and trained staff. The principal aim is that of ensuring and maintaining a high level of awareness of hygiene risks amongst food handlers and other staff who may have indirect contact with food.

Chapter I – general requirements for food premises (other than those specified in Chapter III)

Chapter I lays down the general requirements for ensuring the hygiene of premises in terms of cleaning, maintenance, layout, design, construction and size. It also covers welfare amenity provisions (sanitary accommodation, washing and clothing storage facilities) and environmental provisions (temperature, lighting, ventilation), which should be read in conjunction with comparable provisions under the Workplace (Health, Safety and Welfare) Regulations 1992.

General requirement for food premises
Food premises must be kept clean and maintained in good repair and condition (paragraph 1).

Layout, design, construction and size of food premises
The basic obligation in para 1 of Chapter I is extended in para 2 which requires compliance with four specific requirements. The layout, design, construction and size of food premises must:
(1) permit adequate cleaning and/or disinfection;
(2) be protected against the accumulation of dirt, contact with toxic materials, the shedding of particles into food and the formation of condensation or undesirable mould on surfaces;
(3) permit good food hygiene practices, including protection against cross contamination between and during operations, by foodstuffs, equipment, materials, water, air supply or personnel and external sources of contamination such as pests. (The DoH guidance explains that cross contamination has the same effect as contamination and is an alternative term. Contamination or cross contamination may be direct or indirect);
(4) provide, where necessary, suitable temperature conditions for the hygienic processing and storage of products. (DoH guidance states that suitable temperature conditions are conditions which will keep food safe. The factors to consider are those which may cause a risk to public health. In a catering operation, for example, these may be the holding times and temperature of the food).

In relation to para 2 as a whole, the DoH guidance explains that it is not always necessary to prove that contamination has actually taken place for a breach of the paragraph to occur. The offence, however, will clearly need to be proved and this will require reasonable justification as to why conditions in the premises would not allow good hygiene practices.

Provision of washbasins

There must be an adequate number of washbasins which are suitably located and designated for cleaning hands (para 3). Whether a wash basin is, 'suitably located' is a question of fact depending on the circumstances of the particular business (see *Adams v Flook*, 27 October 1986 (unreported but referred to in BLFD 2729.2) where it was held that whether a wash-hand basin situated on the first floor above a shop was 'conveniently accessible' was a question of fact for magistrates to decide on the evidence before them). DoH guidance explains that designation of wash hand basins does not preclude the use of wash hand basins for other purposes although any such other purposes must be consistent with the requirements of Sched 1. Designation for hand washing means that the basins will be suitable for that purpose and that staff are made aware of the purpose of the wash hand basins. A notice or sign may sometimes be a good means of achieving this, but is not a specific requirement.

Washbasins for cleaning hands must be provided with hot and cold (or appropriately mixed) running water, materials for cleaning hands and for hygienic drying (para 4). These are separate requirements so care should be taken to ensure that summonses are not bad for duplicity (see Chapter 5 and also *Berni Inns Ltd v Reynolds*, 27 March 1981, DC, unreported but referred to in BLFD 2729.1).

Where necessary, the provisions for washing food must be separate from the hand-washing facility (para 4). The need for separate provisions for washing food will depend on whether it is necessary to ensure food safety and wholesomeness. A separate facility need not necessarily mean a separate room or area (see DoH guidance).

Lavatories

An adequate number of flush lavatories must be available and connected to an effective drainage system. Lavatories must not lead directly into rooms in which food is handled (para 3).

Ventilation

There must be suitable and sufficient means of natural or mechanical ventilation. Mechanical air flow from a contaminated area to a clean area must be avoided. Ventilation systems must be so constructed as to enable filters and other parts requiring cleaning or replacement to be readily accessible (para 5). Lavatories within food premises must have adequate natural or mechanical ventilation (para 6).

Lighting, drainage and changing facilities
Food premises must have adequate natural and/or artificial lighting (para 7). Drainage facilities must be adequate for the purpose intended; they must be designed and constructed to avoid the risk of contamination of foodstuffs (para 8) and adequate changing facilities for personnel must be provided where necessary (para 9).

Chapter II – specific requirements in rooms where food is prepared treated or processed.

Chapter II lays down more specific requirements for food manufacturing, preparation and treatment areas and rooms. These requirements apply to all rooms where food is prepared, treated or processed, except for dining rooms, that is, rooms where food is served to people who will consume it there and to premises covered by Chapter III (temporary, domestic premises etc.) Accordingly, the provisions of this Chapter do not apply to rooms in which food is stored, such as cellars.

Floor surfaces
Floor surfaces must be maintained in a sound condition and they must be easy to clean and, where necessary, disinfect. This will require the use of impervious, non-absorbent, washable and non-toxic materials, unless the proprietor of the food business can satisfy the food authority that other materials used are appropriate. Where appropriate, floors must allow adequate surface drainage (para 1(a)). DoH guidance states that 'impervious' means the prevention of initial penetration by moisture. Non-absorbent may require more than the prevention of initial penetration but could also on the other hand be a less stringent requirement in referring to the ability of the material itself to hold water. In practical terms, these requirements are very similar to each other and both apply under paras 1(a) and 1(b) of Chapter II. Very few surfaces are physically 100 per cent impervious, including tile surfaces, and therefore a realistic interpretation should be given to this requirement.

Wall surfaces
Wall surfaces must be maintained in a sound condition and they must be easy to clean and, where necessary, disinfect. This will

require the use of impervious, non-absorbent, washable and non-toxic materials and require a smooth surface up to a height appropriate for the operations, unless the proprietor of the food business can satisfy the food authority that other materials used are appropriate (para 1(b)).

Ceilings and overhead fixtures
Ceilings and overhead fixtures must be designed, constructed and finished to prevent the accumulation of dirt and reduce condensation, the growth of undesirable mould and the shedding of particles (para 1(c)).

Windows
Windows and other openings must be constructed to prevent the accumulation of dirt. Those which can be opened to the outside environment must where necessary be fitted with insect-proof screens which can be easily removed for cleaning. Where open windows would result in the contamination of foodstuffs, windows must remain closed and fixed during production (para 1(d)). DoH guidance makes clear that there is no requirement, implicit or explicit, for sloping window cills to prevent the accumulation of dirt. Where food safety and wholesomeness can be ensured without fly screens, taking into account the nature of the food and the risks involved in the operation, they would not be 'necessary'.

Doors
Doors must be easy to clean and, where necessary, disinfect. This will require the use of smooth and non-absorbent surfaces, unless the proprietor of the food business can satisfy the food authority that other materials used are appropriate (para 1(e)).

Surfaces
Paragraph 1(f) of Chapter II contains a new requirement for surfaces (including surfaces of equipment) which come into contact with food (rather than, 'liable to come into contact', the wording in the Food Hygiene (General) Regulations 1970) to be maintained in a sound condition and be easy to clean and, where necessary, disinfect. Surfaces must be made of smooth, washable and non-toxic materials, unless the proprietor of the food business can satisfy the food authority that other materials used are appropriate. DoH guidance points out that spillages or residues of food (or

ingredients) on a surface will be *de facto* evidence of the fact that the food has come into contact with the surface.

The *Catering Industry Guide* recommends that wooden boards are inappropriate for cutting of high risk foods because wooden boards are not impervious and cannot be cleaned effectively.

Disinfection facilities for equipment

Where necessary, adequate facilities must be provided for the cleaning and disinfecting of work tools and equipment. These facilities must be constructed of materials resistant to corrosion and must be easy to clean and have an adequate supply of hot and cold water (para 2). DoH guidance states that, 'resistant to corrosion' should not be interpreted as a requirement for stainless steel only.

Washing facilities for food

Where appropriate, adequate provision must be made for any necessary washing of the food. Every sink or other such facility must have an adequate supply of hot and/or cold potable water as required, and be kept clean (para 3).

Chapter III – requirements for movable and/or temporary premises

Chapter III covers the majority of the requirements formerly contained in the Food Hygiene (Markets, Stalls and Delivery Vehicles) Regulations 1966. It also extends the scope of food hygiene legislation to vending machines, operations carried out in private houses, such as sandwich preparation, and to village halls and other non-food premises used occasionally for catering purposes where, in the past, enforcement action was either difficult or not possible.

The requirements in Chapter III recognise that, on a practical level, less stringent criteria need to be applied to these types of premises. Accordingly, the basic obligation to site, design, construct and keep clean and maintain premises in good repair and condition in order to avoid the risk of contaminating food and harbouring pests, must be performed, 'so far as is reasonably practicable' (para 1). It is for the prosecution to prove that measures they consider should have been implemented at the premises were reasonably practicable.

The basic obligation is particularised in para 2, with the proviso that the listed matters apply 'where necessary'. There may need to be appropriate facilities to maintain adequate personal hygiene (eg hygienic washing and drying of hands, hygienic sanitary arrangements and changing facilities (para 2(a)). Surfaces which are in contact with food should be in a sound condition and easy to clean and, where necessary, disinfect. Surfaces should be made of smooth, washable, non-toxic materials, unless the proprietor of the food business can satisfy the food authority that other materials used are appropriate (para 2(b)). Adequate provision should be made for cleaning and, where necessary, disinfecting of work utensils and equipment (para 2(c)) and cleaning foodstuffs (para 2(d)). There must be an adequate supply of hot and cold potable water (para 2(e)). Whether automatic vending machines require water depends on what they dispense. As the requirement is for potable water to be supplied, 'where necessary', so long as food safety is not affected, potable water need not be available. Current industry codes of practice, such as the *Technical Handbook* issued by the Automatic Vending Machine Association of Britain (AVAB) already give adequate guidance on this issue. There should also be available adequate arrangements and/or facilities for the hygienic storage and disposal of hazardous and/or inedible substances and waste (whether liquid or solid) (para 2(f)). As with food premises generally, there is a requirement to have available adequate facilities and/or arrangements for maintaining and monitoring suitable food temperature conditions (para 2(g)). Finally, foodstuffs must be so placed as to avoid, so far as is reasonably practicable, the risk of contamination (para 2(h)).

Chapter IV – transport

The FSGFHR recognise the importance of maintaining hygiene standards during the transportation of food. Any vehicle used to transport food (a 'conveyance') must be kept clean and maintained in good repair and condition in order to protect foodstuffs from contamination, and must, where necessary, be designed and constructed to permit adequate cleaning and/or disinfection (para 1). Receptacles in vehicles and/or containers (eg trolleys, trays, crates) must not be used for transporting anything other than foodstuffs where this may result in contamination of foodstuffs (para 2(1)). Likewise the receptacles and/or containers and/or tankers in which foodstuffs are transported in bulk in liquid, granular or powder form must be reserved only for the transport of foodstuffs if otherwise there is a risk of contamination. These containers must be marked in a clearly visible and indelible fashion, in one or more Community languages, to show that they are used for the transport of foodstuffs, or must be marked, 'for foodstuffs only' (para 2(2)). Sometimes materials will be transported with the food which may cause contamination or high and low risk foods are transported in the same vehicle. Where this is the case, products must be effectively separated, where necessary, to protect against the risk of contamination (para 2(3)). In addition, there must be effective cleaning between loads to avoid the risk of contamination (para 2(4)). The food itself must be so placed and protected as to minimise the risk of contamination (para 2(5)). This may involve wrapping the food or storing different foodstuffs in different parts of the vehicle or in separate containers. Where necessary, there must be appropriate temperature control and a system designed to allow temperatures to be monitored (para 2(6)).

Chapter V – equipment requirements

Inadequate cleaning of equipment used for the preparation of food can result in cross-contamination from one foodstuff to another. Paragraph 1 of the FSGFHR requires food businesses to keep clean all articles, fittings and equipment with which food comes into contact. 'Contact' should be given its ordinary and natural meaning in view of the particular facts of the case. It may include not only direct contact but also cases where the food is in such close proximity to the equipment that contamination can occur. How much cleaning a piece of equipment will need depends on its use. For example, a meat slicer is likely to require cleaning (and even disinfection) after every use to avoid cross contamination. Equipment must be so constructed, be of such materials, and be kept in such good order, repair and condition, as to minimise any risk of contamination of the food (para 1(a)). 'Materials' is not defined and it will be a question of fact whether a particular material does minimise contamination risks. Apart from non-returnable containers and packaging, their construction and materials must be maintained in a state to enable them to be thoroughly cleaned and, where necessary, disinfected, sufficient for the purposes intended (para 1(b)). They must be installed in such a manner as to allow adequate cleaning of the surrounding area (para 1(c)).

Chapter VI – food waste

Food businesses necessarily create a great deal of waste which potentially can pose a hazard to food. Chapter VI lays down requirements to minimise any food safety risk. Inevitably, food processing will create so-called, 'working debris' (eg vegetable peelings). It may not be feasible to remove such debris immediately it is created. These practicalities are recognised by Chapter VI, para 1 of which provides that food waste and other refuse must not be allowed to accumulate in food rooms, except so far as is unavoidable for the proper functioning of the business. Appropriately constructed closable containers, which must be kept in sound condition and, where necessary, must be easy to clean and disinfect must be used unless the proprietor of the food business can satisfy the food authority that other types of containers used are appropriate (para 2). The type of container used will depend on the food operation, the use to which the container is put and where it is situated. For example, in relation to the catering industry, the *Catering Industry Guide to the FSGFHR* recognises that lids on containers can themselves be a source of contamination as they are frequently touched by food handlers. Consequently, the *Guide* recommends that containers used for temporary storage of waste in food preparation areas should not have lids but that containers used to store waste must be lidded. There must be procedures for the adequate removal and storage of food waste and other refuse. Refuse stores must be designed and managed in such a way as to enable them to be kept clean, and to protect against access by pests, and against contamination of food, drinking water, equipment or premises (para 3).

Chapter VII – water supply

The quality of water used in food businesses is now prescribed by paragraph 1 of Chapter VII which requires there to be an adequate supply of, 'potable water' which must be used whenever necessary to ensure foodstuffs are not contaminated. 'Potable water' is defined at length in reg 2(1) the principal point of which is that potable water is water which does not adversely affect the wholesomeness of a particular foodstuff in its finished form.

Where appropriate, ice must be made from potable water. The ice must be used whenever necessary to ensure foodstuffs are not contaminated. It must be made, handled and stored under conditions which protect it from all contamination (para 2). Steam used directly in contact with food must not contain any substance which presents a hazard to health, or is likely to contaminate the product (para 3). Potable water will need to be used if the steam comes into contact with food. Water which is unfit for drinking and which is used to generate steam, in refrigeration, fire fighting and other similar purposes not relating to food, must be conducted in separate systems. These must be readily identifiable and must not be connected with, or have the possibility of reflux into, the potable water systems (para 4).

Chapter VIII – personal hygiene

Chapter VIII states the legal requirements designed to achieve 'clean person' strategies. Personnel have two legal obligations. First, every person working in a food handling area must maintain a high degree of personal cleanliness and must wear suitable, clean and, where appropriate, protective clothing (para 1). It is the duty of the proprietor of the food business to ensure that his staff comply with this obligation (reg 4(2)(d)). Accordingly, it is the proprietor who commits an offence where para 1 is breached. It is possible for the food handler to be prosecuted where the commission of the offence was caused by the act or default of the food handler by virtue of the application of s 20 of the FSA to the FSGFHR (see reg 7(c)). The implications of para 1 are wide, as DoH guidance makes clear. Personal cleanliness in this context is intended to include personal hygiene issues such as the need for hand washing and the need to refrain from smoking in food handling areas. Eating, drinking and smoking all involve hand to mouth contact which will compromise the high degree of personal cleanliness required of persons working in a food handling area.

Secondly, reg 5 obliges persons working in food handling areas who either know or suspect that they are suffering from, or are a carrier of, a disease likely to be transmitted through food or who have, for example, an infected wound, skin infection, sores or diarrhoea, to report the condition to the proprietor of the food business. Paragraph 2 of Chapter VIII obliges the proprietor to exclude that person from working in any food handling area in any capacity in which there is any likelihood of that person directly or indirectly contaminating food with pathogenic micro-organisms. If the proprietor fails to exclude the food handler, he commits an offence.

Chapter IX – provisions applicable to foodstuffs

Food businesses must not accept any raw materials or ingredients if they are known to be, or might reasonably be expected to be, so contaminated with parasites, pathogenic micro-organisms, or toxic, decomposed or foreign substances, that after normal sorting and/or preparatory or processing procedures hygienically applied by food businesses, they would still be unfit for human consumption (para 1). This paragraph reflects the principle adopted by the Divisional Court in *R v Southampton Justices, ex p. Barrow Lane & Ballard Ltd* [1983] (unreported) namely, that product which is contaminated may be rendered wholesome by a process to which it is subjected. In order to avoid commission of an offence under this paragraph, food businesses will need to operate procedures by which food which has the potential to be contaminated is identified and excluded from use. Such procedures could include routine checks of deliveries of product.

Once raw materials and ingredients are on the premises they must be stored in appropriate conditions designed to prevent harmful deterioration and to protect them from contamination (para 2).

Paragraph 3 of Chapter IX requires foodstuffs which are handled, stored, packaged, displayed and transported, to be protected against any contamination likely to render the food unfit for human consumption, injurious to health or contaminated in such a way that it would be unreasonable to expect it to be consumed in that state. In particular, food must be so placed and/or protected as to minimise any risk of contamination. This does not mean that the business must prevent any and all levels of contamination (DoH guidance). The requirements of paragraph 3 mirror the provisions of s 8(2) of the FSA (discussed in detail in Chapter 3, p 25) which lists the 'food safety requirements' with which food businesses must comply. The prosecution must be able to prove beyond reasonable doubt that there is a risk of contamination of the food likely to render it unfit, injurious to health, or make it unreasonable to expect it to be consumed. For an example of challenging prosecution evidence to this effect, see the discussion on sneeze screens earlier in this chapter (pp 48–9). In the case of food poisoning bacteria, the way in which food is handled, stored, displayed and transported should be designed to minimise any initial risk of contamination as well as preventing the proliferation of bacteria to harmful levels. Evidence called in food poisoning cases relating to, 'cook-chill' foods frequently centres on the latter, in particular whether the food was cooked rapidly enough to prevent or minimise growth in bacteria and/or whether it was reheated to a sufficiently high temperature to eradicate bacteria (eg cooking chicken which harbours salmonella bacteria).

The food business must also have adequate procedures to ensure that pests are controlled (para 3). According to DoH guidance, controlling pests includes eradication of pests where possible. The intention is to ensure that premises are kept free of all pests, where they could contaminate food. In order to achieve this there must be procedures in place which will prevent pests from entering the premises or, if they are present, eradicate them. Chapter I, para 2(c) is also relevant for the design and layout of premises, which should permit protection against pests, eg by physical proofing. Adequate procedures do not necessarily imply specialist pest control contracts. Whilst pest control contracts may be one way of fulfilling the requirement, the need for them must be assessed according to the level of risk. Effective in-house control procedures could satisfy this requirement.

Hazardous and/or inedible substances, including animal feedstuffs, must be adequately labelled and stored in separate and secure containers (para 4). Food which has become inedible due to spoilage should be kept separately and labelled 'not for human consumption' before disposal.

Chapter X – training

An important new requirement of the FSGFHR is that proprietors must ensure that food handlers are supervised and instructed and/or trained in food hygiene matters commensurate with their work activities (para 1). 'Food handler' is not defined in the FSGFHR. DoH guidance says that it means a person who handles food in the course of their work as part of their duties. *The Catering Industry's Guide to Good Hygiene Practice* defines it as 'any person involved in a food business who handles or prepares food (which includes drink and ice) whether open (unwrapped) or packaged'. These interpretations are guidance only and cannot be legally binding. Whether someone is a food handler is likely to be a question of fact for a court ultimately to decide on the evidence before it.

Whilst organisations such as the Chartered Institute of Environmental Health have made great strides in promoting general food hygiene training over the last twenty years, food hygiene training must now be more directed to the food hazards identified from the risk assessment process of HACCP. Many small food businesses have neither the expertise nor resources to undertake this exercise. The question of the high levels of part-time and casual labour employed in certain sectors of the food industry will also need consideration as far as training is concerned.

DoH guidance recommends that, in any initial assessment of training, instruction or supervision needs, a general and comprehensive approach should be adopted. Existing guidance issued by the food industry suggests that the term 'food handler' should encompass any factory operators, shop assistants, catering staff and includes volunteers and staff recruited temporarily. This does not necessarily mean that all these staff will need food hygiene training. The requirement is for supervision, instruction and/or training commensurate with their work activities.

Training implies that recipients will have a greater level of understanding at the end of the process than if they were simply provided with instruction. The distinction does have a bearing on the subsequent supervision required. Where training is a requirement, a decision needs to be made on the level of initial training required for the type of task being undertaken, followed by refresher training at intervals.

Instruction is likely to require a person to be made aware initially and, where appropriate, routinely, of what needs to be done, usually for a range of simpler tasks involving lower risk foods, and where formal training is not required. In some circumstances, instruction with supervision of an intensive kind can substitute for training, eg where there is a high staff turnover. In some situations also, instruction may be followed up by more formal training at a later date to reduce the level of supervision required.

Food Safety (Temperature Control) Regulations 1995

The Food Safety (Temperature Control) Regulations 1995 (FSTCR) implement paras 4 and 5 of Chapter IX of the Annex to the Council Directive 93/43/EEC of 14 June 1993 on the hygiene of foodstuffs, as well as containing certain national provisions relating to food temperature control. They revoke in their entirety the Food Hygiene (Amendment) Regulations 1990 and the Food Hygiene

(Amendment) Regulations 1991 which concerned temperature control.

The FSTCR should be read in conjunction with the Food Safety (General Food Hygiene) Regulations (FSGFHR) 1995. They are accompanied by Guidance on The Food Safety (Temperature Control) Regulations 1995 issued by the Department of Health (DoH) which is available from HMSO. *Code of Practice No 10: Enforcement of the Temperature Control Requirements of Food Hygiene Regulations* is currently being revised by the DoH. It still, however, provides guidance on accurate measurement of temperature and procedures to be followed to ensure accuracy.

The FSTCR regulate the temperature of the foodstuff itself, not its surrounding air temperature. It is vital that this important distinction is borne in mind when dealing with any criminal prosecution under the FSTCR.

To what industries and businesses do the FSTCR apply?

Apart from a number of exempted industries, the FSTCR applies across all industry sectors. The exempted industries are, first, primary production which includes harvesting, slaughter and milking (reg 2(1)) and, secondly, to the fish, live mollusc, egg, meat, poultry and dairy industries where specific regulations listed in reg 3(2) apply (although, in relation to the fishing industry, the FSTCR will apply to activities governed by regulations listed in reg 3(2) unless those regulations specifically prescribe additional or alternative temperature control methods).

The FSTCR contains the same definition of 'food business' as in the FSGFHR, that is, 'any undertaking, whether carried on for profit or not and whether public or private, carrying out any or all of the following operations, namely, preparation, processing, manufacture, packaging, storage, transportation, distribution, handling or offering for sale or supply, of food'. The extended meaning of, 'sale' given in s 2 of the FSA applies to the FSTCR (reg 18(a)).

Offences created by the FSTCR and applicable defences (England and Wales)

Six separate offences are created by Pt II of the FSTCR. The s 21 of the FSA defence of 'due diligence' applies to all those offences (reg 18(d)) as do the provisions of section 20 of the FSA (offences due to the fault of another person (reg 18(c)). The FSA defences are discussed in detail in Chapter 5. There are also specific defences created by the FSTCR which are available to defendants charged for offences under the FSTCR which are considered in this chapter.

Failure to keep food below 8°C

It is an offence for any person to keep any food (except for food supplied by mail order (reg 4(2)) and subject to certain exemptions listed on page 65 below) which is likely to support the growth of pathogenic micro-organisms or the formation of toxins and with respect to which any commercial operation is being carried out, at or in food premises at a temperature above 8°C (reg 4(1)). This is an offence of strict liability.

Neither 'commercial operation' nor 'food premises' is defined in the FSTCR.

Statutory defences

The complexities of the food industry are recognised by the provision in the FSTCR of two statutory defences, upward variation of temperature and chill holding tolerance periods. The first, upward variation of temperature, is set out in reg 6. The defendant must prove four factors. First, that a food business which is responsible for manufacturing, preparing or processing of food recommended that the food be kept at or below a specified temperature between 8°C and ambient temperatures ('the recommended temperature') for a period not exceeding a specified shelf life (which is defined in reg 2(1), in effect the 'use by' or 'best before' date). Secondly, where the defendant is not the recommending food business, that the recommendation was communicated to the defendant either on a label or another appropriate means of written instruction. Thirdly, that the food was kept within the recommended temperature parameters and fourthly, that the food was not kept beyond the specified shelf life.

The second defence – chill holding tolerance periods – recognises the difficulties in maintaining temperature at or below 8°C in certain circumstances. Many hotels and restaurants have buffet displays of cold food such as meat, fish, salads and desserts. These displays are on offer to the customer during set lunch and dinner periods. It is a defence under reg 7(1) for a defendant to prove that the food: was for service or on display for sale; had not previously been kept for service or on display for sale at a temperature above 8°C or, in appropriate circumstances, the recommended temperature; and had been kept for service or on display for sale for a period of less than four hours.

Food should be removed from sale where it has been on display for four hours or more. The FSTCR do not specify what should happen to the food thereafter. However, since one of the components of the defence is to prove that the food had not previously been kept for service or displayed, it is submitted that any leftover food which had not been kept below 8°C cannot be served again and must be destroyed.

The food industry has to transport a substantial amount of ready-chilled foodstuffs and there may be an increase in the temperature of the food during loading and unloading. Under reg 7(2)(a) it is a defence to prove that the food was being transferred

(i)   to a vehicle used for the purposes of the activities of a food business from; or

(ii) from a vehicle used for the purposes of the activities of a food business to

premises (which includes vehicles) at which the food was going to be kept at or below 8°C or, in appropriate circumstances, the recommended temperature.

Sometimes it becomes impossible for the food to be kept at the desired temperature. It is a defence under reg 7(2)(b) to prove that the food was kept at a temperature above 8°C or, in appropriate circumstances, the recommended temperature for an unavoidable reason, such as

(a)   to accommodate the practicalities of handling during and after processing or preparation;

(b)   the defrosting of equipment; or

(c)   temporary breakdown of equipment,

and that the food was kept at or above 8°C or, in appropriate circumstances, the recommended temperature for a limited period only which period was consistent with food safety.

Supplying food by mail order which has given or is likely to give rise to a risk to health

It is an offence for any person to supply by mail order any food which is likely to support the growth of pathogenic micro-organisms or the formation of toxins and is being or has been conveyed by post or by a private or common carrier to an ultimate consumer, at a temperature which has given rise to or is likely to give rise to a risk to health (reg 4(3)). 'Ultimate consumer' means any person who buys otherwise than: for the purpose of resale; for the purpose of a catering establishment or for the purpose of a manufacturing business.

Exemptions to the requirements of keeping food below 8°C and not supplying food by mail order which poses a risk to health
Regulation 5 provides that regulation 4 does not apply to the following:
  (a) cooked or reheated food which is for service or on display for sale and which needs to be kept hot in order to control the growth of pathogenic micro-organisms or the formation of toxins;
  (b) food which, for the duration of its shelf life, may be kept at ambient temperatures with no risk to health;
  (c) food which is being or has been subjected to a process such as dehydration or canning intended to prevent the growth of pathogenic micro-organisms at ambient temperatures. When a hermetically sealed container is opened, the food must be kept at or below 8°C;
  (d) food which must be ripened or matured at ambient temperatures. Once the food has ripened or matured, it must be kept at or below 8°C;
  (e) raw food intended for further processing (which includes cooking) before human consumption, but only if that processing, if undertaken correctly, will render that food fit for human consumption;
  (f) food to which Council Regulation (EEC) No 1906/90 on certain marketing standards for poultry, as amended, applies;
  (g) food to which Council Regulation (EEC) No 1907/90 on certain marketing standards for eggs, as amended, applies.

Recommending a temperature above 8°C without a supporting well-founded scientific assessment
It is an offence for a food business to make an upward variation of temperature recommendation without it being supported by a well-founded scientific assessment of the safety of the food at the specified temperature (reg 6(2)). When considering whether there is a risk to food safety, regard must be had to the nature of the food, the manner in which it is handled and packed, any process to which the food is subjected before supply to the consumer, and the

conditions under which it is displayed or stored (reg 2(2)). A scientific assessment contained in a guide to good hygiene practice which has been approved by the Minister under the art 5 procedures of the Council Directive 93/43/EEC of 14 June 1993 on the hygiene of foodstuffs will be considered sufficient evidence that it is well-founded, unless the contrary is proved (reg 12). The burden of proof will be on the prosecution to demonstrate that any scientific assessment contained in such a guide was not sufficient. Scientific assessments incorporated in guides to good hygiene practice issued by the DoH are a new concept in food hygiene law. It is envisaged that such guides will be produced on an on-going basis to support the requirements of the regulations.

Keeping hot food below 63°C
Food poisoning bacteria can proliferate in food which is warmed to inadequate temperatures. Regulation 8 makes it an offence for any person in the course of the activities of a food business to keep any food which:
(a) has been cooked or reheated;
(b) is for service or on display for sale; and
(c) needs to be kept hot in order to control the growth of pathogenic micro-organisms or the formation of toxins, at or in food premises at a temperature below 63°C.
Statutory defence. There are two statutory defences available to defendants charged under reg 8. Both defences apply to circumstances where the food is kept hot in hot cabinets in the kitchen before service or in hot holding buffet displays. Under reg 9(1), the defendant must prove two facts:
(a) that there was a well-founded scientific assessment of the safety of the food which concluded that there was no risk to health from holding for service or on a display for sale the cooked or reheated food at a temperature below 63°C for a specified period of time which was not exceeded; and
(b) that at the time the offence was alleged to have been committed, the food was held in a manner which was justified in the light of that scientific assessment.
Under reg 9(2), the defendant must prove that the food had been kept for service or on display for sale for a period of less than two hours and had not previously been kept for service or on display for sale by that person. This means that food which has been kept hot for more than two hours cannot be re-used.

In practice, a defendant will have to rely on the reg 9(1) defence where he holds hot food at less than 63°C for a period of more than two hours and even then only where a scientific assessment supports holding the food for a longer specified period.

Keeping any food at temperatures which would result in a risk to health

Regulation 10(1) contains an offence which applies to all foodstuffs. It is an offence for any person in the course of the activities of a food business to keep raw materials, ingredients, intermediate products or finished products which are likely to support the growth of pathogenic micro-organisms or the formation of toxins at temperatures which would result in a risk to health. The burden of proof is on the prosecution to show that there is a risk to health.

Some temperature control tolerance is allowed by reg 10(2) which permits limited periods outside temperature control where these are necessary to accommodate the practicalities of handling during preparation, transport, storage, display and service of food, so long as this is consistent with food safety.

Manufacturers frequently give special storage instructions for chilled foods to be kept at temperatures below 8°C. Where the special storage instructions are not complied with an offence may be committed even though technically there is compliance with regs 4 and 8 (reg 10(3)). In most circumstances, food businesses complying with the more specific requirement for a maximum temperature of 8°C will also be complying with reg 10(1). The question would be whether there is a risk to health in keeping the food at a different temperature.

Failing to cool food quickly to the required temperature

It is an offence for any food business responsible for cooling any food which must be kept below ambient temperature not to cool that food as quickly as possible after the final heat processing stage or if no heat process is applied, the final preparation stage, to the temperature at which it must be kept under the FSTCR.

Offences created by the FSTCR applicable in Scotland

Part III of the FSTCR creates in relation to Scotland four offences.

Failing to keep food in a refrigerator or at a temperature above 63°C

Under reg 13(1), all except certain exempted foods on or in food premises and in respect of which commercial operations are being carried out must either be kept in a refrigerator or refrigerating chamber or in a cool, ventilated place or at a temperature above 63°C.

The exempted foods are:

(a) foods which are being prepared for sale;

(b) food which is exposed for sale or has been sold to a consumer, whether for immediate consumption or otherwise;

(c) food which, immediately following any process of cooking to which it is subjected or the final processing stage if no cooking process is applied, is being cooled under hygienic conditions as quickly as possible to a temperature which would not result in a risk to health;

(d) food which, in order that it may be conveniently available for sale on the premises to consumers, it is reasonable to keep otherwise than as referred to in reg 13(1);

(e) food which, for the duration of its shelf life, may be kept at ambient temperatures with no risk to health;

(f) food to which Council Regulation (EEC) No 1906/90 on certain marketing standards for poultry, as amended, applies;

(g) food to which Council Regulation (EEC) No 1907/90 on certain marketing standard for eggs, as amended, applies.

Failing to reheat food to not less than 82°C

Where food has already been cooked, it must be reheated to a temperature of not less than 82°C before it is served for immediate consumption or exposed for sale (reg 14(1)).

Statutory defence. It is a defence for the person charged to prove that he could not have raised the food to a temperature of not less than 82°C without a deterioration of its qualities (reg 14(2)).

Failing to boil gelatine to a temperature of not less than 71°C for 30 minutes

Regulation 15(1) provides that gelatine intended for use in bakers' confectionery filling, meat products or fish products in the course of the activities of a food business must, immediately before use, be brought to the boil or brought to and kept at a temperature of not less than 71°C for 30 minutes.

Any gelatine left over after completion of the process must, if not treated as waste, be cooled under hygienic conditions as quickly as is reasonably practicable. When it is cold it must be kept in a refrigerator or a refrigerating chamber or a cool ventilated place (reg 15(2)).

Keeping any food at temperatures which would result in a risk to health

Regulation 16 creates an offence virtually identical to that in reg 10(1) which is discussed above. The only difference is that reg 16(3) exempts food which, immediately following a final heat processing stage, or a final preparation stage if no heat process is applied, is being cooled as quickly as possible to a temperature which would not result in a risk to health. Limited temperature tolerance periods are permitted where these are consistent with food safety (reg 16(3)).

Penalties

Offences created by regs 4, 6(2), 8, 10, 11, 13, 14, 15 and 16 are triable either way. The penalty on summary conviction is a maximum fine of not more than £5,000. The penalty on conviction on indictment is an unlimited fine or imprisonment for a term not exceeding two years or both. Section 34 of the FSA (time limit for prosecutions) (referred to in Chapter 5, pp 72–4) applies to these offences and also to offences committed by bodies corporate under s 36 of the FSA which applies to the FSTCR, subject to the modifications listed in reg 18(h).

Enforcement of the FSTCR

The FSTCR are enforced by the food authority of the area in which the alleged offence is committed, that is, district councils or county councils in the case of unitary authorities (see reg 19(1) and the definition of 'food authority' in reg 2(1)).

The food authority has a duty to inspect food premises with a frequency commensurate with the risks associated with those premises. In enforcing the FSTCR, due consideration must be given to whether the business complied with approved industry guides to good hygiene practice (reg 19(2)(b)).

Methods of enforcement of the FSGFHR and the FSTCR

A number of enforcement methods are available to enforcement officers, ranging from informal letters detailing breaches of legal requirements, to use of the statutory methods of enforcement (improvement notices and emergency prohibition notices) to prosecution in the courts. Enforcement officers are advised in the *Code of Practice No 2: Legal Matters* and in *Code of Practice No 9: Food Hygiene Inspection* (revised September 1995) to adopt a graduated approach to enforcement, depending on various factors including the business's history of compliance and the relative seriousness of any identified breaches of the regulations. The graduated approach to enforcement is discussed in detail in Chapter 8. The factors to consider before deciding to prosecute are listed in Chapter 3.

Advising the client

To the defendant, many allegations of breach of food hygiene regulations look impossible to defend. Undoubtedly, because they create offences of strict liability, it can be difficult to mount a defence. However, it is important when advising a client on any enforcement action taken under the FSGFHR and the FSTCR always to consider three principal avenues of defence. First, there may be a technical defect in the manner in which enforcement action was commenced. For example, in relation to prosecutions in the Magistrates Court, one or more of the technical defences discussed in Chapter 5 may apply. Chapter 8 considers in detail the procedural requirements of statutory methods of enforcement with which enforcement authorities must comply in order for those methods to be valid.

Secondly, where technical defences are not available, consideration should be given to whether the enforcement authority has sufficient evidence to prove its accusation beyond reasonable doubt. This is likely to involve discussing in detail with the client the facts alleged by the enforcing authority and investigating the accuracy of those facts. The client or his staff may have accompanied the enforcement officer on the inspection which led to the accusation being made and may have contemporaneous notes which paint a different picture of conditions at the premises at the time of the inspection. Alternatively, eye witness accounts may have to be taken. Such investigations can be time consuming and therefore expensive in terms of legal costs so it is advisable initially to explore with the instructing client whether there is any reasonable prospect of challenging accusations on factual grounds before embarking on lengthy investigations. Once the facts are available, the next step should be a careful analysis of the wording of the relevant regulation which it is alleged the client has breached. There may be scope to challenge the enforcement officer's interpretation of the regulation, particularly in the case of the provisions of the FSGFHR which use subjective terms such as, 'where necessary'; 'where appropriate', 'suitable', 'adequate' etc.

Thirdly, in the case of prosecutions or appeals against improvement notices where there is *prima facie* evidence that the relevant offence was committed, consideration must be given to whether a 'due diligence' defence may be available to the client. Chapter 5 discusses the legal aspects of that defence in detail (pp 80–81). As a practical matter, the defence solicitor handling a case under the FSGFHR and the FSTCR is likely to be involved in scrutinising the business systems relevant to the particular accusation in order to assess the viability of a due diligence defence. All written documentation pertaining to the relevant part of the system should be considered. However, it is not a legal requirement for businesses to have written procedures. Possibly, the existence of relevant procedures and the fact that they were implemented and monitored could be proved by oral testimony.

In preparing any defence, regard should be had to any relevant codes of practice, industry guides and government guidance notes. It may be worthwhile contacting LACOTS to ascertain whether it has provided advice to enforcement officers since *Code of Practice No 9: Food Hygiene Inspections* (revised September 1995) recommends to officers that they should heed any such advice.

Further advice

Further advice on determining food shelf lives may be found in the following publications: *Shelf Life of Foods – Guidelines for its Determination and Prediction* – Institute of Food Science and Technology (UK) – ISBN 0 905367 11 1 (Available from Institute of Food Science and Technology (UK), 5 Cambridge Court, 210 Shepherds Bush Road, London W6 7NL). *Evaluation of Shelf Life for Chilled Foods – Campden and Chorleywood Food Research Association, Technical Manual No 28* (Available from Campden Food Research Association, Chipping Campden, Gloucestershire GL55 6LD).

Chapter 5

Defences

Introduction

Most technical defences argued in food safety cases concern procedural rules for the commencement and conduct of proceedings in the Magistrates' Court. For a comprehensive review of procedural matters in the Magistrates' Court, see *Stones Justices Manual*. The defences considered below are those most commonly cited in food cases. Technical defences relating to the methods of enforcement available to food authorities are considered in Chapter 8.

Time limits

Apart from one exception (the offence of obstruction of officers under s 33(1) of the FSA for which the time limit is six months, (Magistrates' Courts Act 1980, s 127), food prosecutions must be commenced before the expiry of three years from the commission of the offence or one year from its discovery by the prosecutor, whichever is the earlier (FSA, s 34).

The rules relating to when an information is laid before the Magistrates are relevant to calculating whether the prosecutor has complied with s 34 (see Chapter 3, pp 14–15).

In *R v Thames Metropolitan Stipendiary Magistrate ex p the London Borough of Hackney* [1993] 158 JP 305, the Divisional Court held that offences created by the Food Hygiene (General) Regulations 1970 ('the 1970 Regulations') were continuing offences committed afresh each day that the Regulations were not complied with. Accordingly, where the prosecution discovered offences on 14 September 1989 and on re-inspection on 19 March 1990 found that the defects had not been remedied, an information laid on

15 November 1990 was not out of time because the relevant date for the purposes of the time limit was 19 March 1990.

The 1970 Regulations contained their own time limit provision, reg 95, which was identical to the terms of s 34 of the FSA. The 1970 Regulations have been repealed and replaced by the Food Safety (General Food Hygiene) Regulations 1995. Section 34 applies to the FSGFHR pursuant to reg 7(g). In principle, the FSGFHR also create continuing offences to which the rule in the *Thames Metropolitan Stipendiary Magistrate* case will apply.

Despite the clear wording of s 34, unjustifiable delay in the commencement of a prosecution even within the statutory time limit may constitute an abuse of process of the court. The Magistrates' Court has the power to halt such a prosecution but that power should only be used in the most 'exceptional circumstances' (*Director of Public Prosecutions v Humphrys* [1977] AC 1 p. 26, *per* Viscount Dilhorne; Lord Lane CJ in *Attorney-General's Reference (No 1 of 1990)* [1992] Cr App R 296, 302–303). Abuse of the process of the court may arise where the prosecution manipulates or misuses the process of the court so that the defendant is deprived of a protection provided by the law or has taken unfair advantage of a technicality, or on the balance of probability the defendant has been, or will be, prejudiced in the preparation or conduct of his defence by delay on the part of the prosecution which is unjustifiable (see *R v The Derby Crown Court ex p Brookes* [1985] 80 Cr App R 164 *per* Sir Roger Ormrod; approved by the Divisional Court in *R v Bow Street Stipendiary Magistrate ex p DPP and ex p Cherry* (1989) *The Times*, 20 December).

The defendant must have suffered prejudice as a result of the delay. A failure by the prosecution to disclose the identity of the complainant to the defendant until the information had been laid nine months after the alleged offence was committed constituted such prejudice (*Daventry District Council v Olins* [1990] 154 JP 478, DC; see also *R v Taylor* (1994) *The Times*, 17 August, where the Court of Appeal held that a defendant in a criminal trial had a fundamental right to see and to know the identity of his accusers, including witnesses for the prosecution. The right should only be denied in rare and exceptional circumstances).

However, mere delay does not automatically constitute prejudice. In *South Pembrokeshire District Council v Pitman*, (unreported) overruling the decision of the magistrates, the Divisional Court held that a six-month delay in laying the information after discovery of the alleged offence did not seriously prejudice the defendant. The defendant knew of the nature of the allegations against her the day the alleged food safety offence was committed, 22 April 1993, was interviewed by the food authority the following day, 23 April 1993, received an analyst's report on 13 May 1993 and informed the Council in writing that she had taken action upon the complaint and had sacked a member of staff on 20 May 1993. On 9 June 1993, the Council requested information about ownership of the business from the defendant. In July 1993 the Council decided to prosecute but waited until the requested information arrived on 12 August 1993. On 31 August 1993 local solicitors were instructed to commence the prosecution. They delayed six weeks until 12 October 1993 to lay the information. Whilst the Divisional Court considered that six weeks was an excessive time in which to lay an information, overall the Court did not consider the delay prior to laying the information to be inordinate.

Duplicity

An information and summons must describe in ordinary language the specific offence for which the defendant is charged, giving such particulars as may be necessary to give reasonable information about the nature of the charge (r 100(1) of the Magistrates' Courts Rules 1981).

A Magistrates' Court has no jurisdiction to try an information that charges more than one offence (r 12(1) of the Magistrates' Court Rules 1981). However, it is permissible to set out in one document two or more informations (r 100(2) of the Magistrates' Courts Rules 1981). Non-compliance with these rules is not a mere irregularity but is a matter of substance. If an information is bad for duplicity, justices do not have the jurisdiction to begin the trial and, once the trial has begun, the information cannot be amended (*Hargreaves v Alderson* [1964] 2 QB 159, DC).

An information is bad for duplicity if it charges facts which constitute more than one single activity. Where different acts are components of a single activity, it is permissible to lay one information (*Jemmison v Priddle* [1972] 1 QB 489, where the information charged the killing of two deer and *Horrix v Malam* [1984] RTR 112, where the information charged two sightings of erratic driving within a ten minute period on the same road which were held to be a continuous activity). It is irrelevant that two separate offences are charged in the conjunctive ('and') or disjunctive ('or') form (see

Bastin v Davies [1950] 2 KB 579; *Mallon v Allon* [1964] 1 QB 385; *Ware v Fox; Fox v Dingley* [1967] 1 WLR 379).

Charging offences under the Food Hygiene (General) Regulations 1970 has caused difficulties for prosecutors as illustrated by two cases.

It is not duplicitous for an information to charge five separate offences under the Food Hygiene (General) Regulations 1970 in one document, a preamble to those offences setting out material common to all of them (*Director of Public Prosecutions v Shah* [1984] 1 WLR 886, HL). The fact that in a single document a preamble contained particulars common to a number of otherwise separate allegations did not connect them in such a way as to amount to charging a number of offences in one information.

In *George v Kumar* (1980) 80 LGR 526, the Divisional Court held that, in imposing an obligation to keep the structure of every food room clean, reg 25 of the Food Hygiene (General) Regulations 1970 only created two offences: failing to keep the structure of the food room clean; and failing to keep the structure of the food room in good order, repair and condition. It did not create, as the prosecution argued, a separate offence in respect of each part of the food room mentioned in the preamble to reg 25 which would result in reg 25 creating more than 20 offences.

Whether this case will be followed in the future is debatable now that the Food Hygiene (General) Regulations 1970 have been repealed and replaced by the Food Safety (General Food Hygiene) Regulations 1995. The obligation to keep the structure of premises clean and in good condition is now contained in the various sub-paras of para 1 of Ch II to Sched 1 of the FSGFHR. It is submitted that the effect of para 1 is to create separate offences in respect of each sub-para. Applying *George v Kumar*, it is arguable that each sub-para of para 1 creates in relation to the part of the structure named in the sub-section further separate offences. So, for example, para 1(a) creates two offences:

(a) in relation to the maintenance of floor surfaces in a sound condition; and

(b) in relation to the floor surfaces being easy to keep clean.

The practical consequence of these changes is that prosecutors can now charge a food proprietor with many more separate offences in respect of the structure of food premises, thus exposing the proprietor to potentially far greater financial penalty in the event of conviction.

Identity of the person summoned

Section 123 of the Magistrates' Courts Act 1980 entitles magistrates to correct an error in a summons by amending it. However, magistrates have no power to amend a summons to alter the identity of the defendant originally charged, where the correct defendant was not present in court, understood why the summons was being amended and would suffer no prejudice as a result.

In *Marco (Croydon) Ltd trading as A & J Bull Containers v Metropolitan Police* [1984] RTR 24, the company against which the information was laid was A J Bull Ltd. At the hearing of the information, the prosecution applied for the summons to be amended by substituting Marco (Croydon) Ltd trading as A & J Bull Containers as the defendant. Counsel instructed by A & J Bull Ltd resisted the amendment on the grounds that the two companies were separate legal entities, albeit within the same group of companies. The magistrates decided that the prosecution had correctly identified the defendant but had merely misstated the name of the company and allowed the amendment. The case was adjourned under s 123(2) of the Magistrates' Courts Act 1980 to establish whether counsel was to be instructed by Marco (Croydon) Ltd. He was so instructed, the case proceeded and that company was convicted.

On appeal to the Divisional Court, it was held that, by granting the adjournment, the magistrates had accepted that, until counsel obtained further instructions, he was not instructed by Marco (Croydon) Ltd. Therefore, technically the wrong defendant was before the court and the magistrates had no power to substitute Marco (Croydon) Ltd for A & J Bull Ltd.

Similarly, in *R v Greater Manchester Justices, ex p Aldi GmbH & Co KG* (1994) *The Times*, 28 December, the Divisional Court quashed an amendment of an information made by the magistrates where they substituted Aldi GmbH & Co KB for Aldi Stores Ltd, the company against which the information was originally laid.

Confusion as to the identity of the defendant can be minimised by the prosecutor requesting from the person believed to have committed the offence information as the nature of their interest in the land from which the food business is traded, pursuant to their power to obtain particulars of persons interested in land under s 16 of the Local Government (Miscellaneous Provisions) Act 1976.

Identity of the prosecutor

Responsibility for enforcement of the provisions of the FSA rests with the food authority for the area in which the offence is committed unless otherwise provided by the FSA (s 6(2)). Food authorities are, in practice, the local authority. Accordingly, it is for the local authority to decide to prosecute but often that decision is taken by an enforcement officer or a special committee which is authorised by a resolution of the Council to do so. If the prosecution is commenced by a person not properly authorised by the local authority, the proceedings are invalid (*Snodgrass v Topping* (1952) 116 JP 332; *Oberst v Coombs* (1955) 53 LGR 316; *Campbell v Wallsend Slipway and Engineering Co Ltd* [1978] ICR 1015, DC).

Whether the local authority's enforcement officers conduct prosecutions themselves or leave that to the authority's solicitor, is a matter for the Council of the authority to decide. Section 222 of the Local Government Act 1972 gives a local authority power to prosecute or defend or appear in legal proceedings. Section 223 of that Act provides that any member or officer of a local authority may exercise those powers, as long as he is authorised by the local authority to do so. Local authorities usually pass a resolution giving general authorisation for particular individuals to exercise the powers conferred on the local authority by s 222, thus providing a general delegation of those powers to those authorised. Once authorised, such individuals may act as if they were a certified solicitor even though they may not be qualified solicitors (s 223(1)).

Substantive defences

Prosecutions under food safety law tend to be of two specific types. First, a client may be charged with breaches of the 'food safety' or 'consumer protection' provisions of the FSA. Secondly, as a result of a complaint from a member of the public, or following a routine inspection of food premises by an authorised officer, he may be charged with breaching the general and specific requirements of, for instance, the Food Safety (General Food Hygiene) Regulations 1995.

The four principal offences under the FSA are:

(a) rendering food injurious to health (s 7);
(b) selling food not complying with the food safety requirements (s 8);

    (c) selling food which is not of the nature or substance or quality demanded (s 14); and

    (d) falsely describing or presenting food (s 15).

The more common offences under the FSGFHR include:

    (a) failing to ensure that any of the following operations, namely the preparation, processing, manufacture, packing, storage, transportation, distribution, handling and offering for sale or supply of food are carried out in a hygienic way (reg 4);

    (b) breaches of the 'Rules of Hygiene' detailed in Sched 1 to the Regulations.

Defences

All the duties under both the FSA and FSGFHR are of an absolute nature, that is, no proof of intent is required for an offence to be committed. There are, however, several ways in which the defence can challenge charges involving offences of strict liability.

Proof of the constituent elements of the particular offence

The prosecution must be able to prove beyond reasonable doubt that the defendant committed the offence charged. That necessitates proof of the constituent elements of the relevant offence. For example, where a defendant is charged under s 14 of the FSA with selling food to the prejudice of the purchaser which was not of the quality demanded, the prosecution must establish a 'sale', that such sale prejudiced the purchaser and that the food was not of the quality demanded. Failure to prove all of these elements to the requisite standard of proof is likely to result in a submission by the defence of no case to answer at the conclusion of the prosecution's case.

The fault of another person

Many food offences, particularly those relating to food which is supplied to rather than prepared by the person who has committed the offence, result from an error in production by the manufacturer or supplier of the food. Section 20 of the FSA provides that, 'where the commission by any person of an offence under the preceding provisions of this Part is due to an act or default of some other person, that other person shall be guilty of the offence; and a person may be charged with and convicted of the offence by virtue of this section whether or not proceedings are taken against the first-mentioned person'. The 'preceding provisions' of the FSA are in practice ss 7, 8, 14 and 15.

'Some other person' can include an employee of a company providing that he does not constitute the controlling mind or will of the company (see *Tesco Supermarkets v Nattrass* [1971] 2 All ER 127). A range of individuals could be classed as 'other persons' within the meaning of this section, such as managers involved in food production, catering managers, quality assurance managers and food technologists.

Rather than operating as a defence in the strict sense of the word, this section provides a procedure by which the person really responsible for the commission of the relevant offence may be brought before the court.

A typical example of the use of s 20 would be where a complaint of a foreign body in, say, a loaf of bread is investigated by the enforcement authority. Technically, the retailer who sold the bread to the customer would have committed an offence under s 14 of the FSA. However, where the investigation demonstrates that the foreign body came to be in the loaf as a result of a fault in the production process, s 20 enables the prosecution to charge the manufacturer instead of or in addition to the retailer. Section 20 should be read in conjunction with s 21 (due diligence).

Section 20 should also be considered in conjunction with s 36 of the FSA which provides that, where an offence committed by a body corporate, is proved to have been committed with the consent or connivance of, or attributable to any neglect by, any director, manager, secretary or other similar officer of the body corporate or by any person purporting to act in any such capacity, that person and the body corporate shall be deemed to be guilty of the relevant offence and proceedings can be taken against both.

Guidance as to who is a 'manager' under s 36 can be found in *Tesco Supermarkets Ltd v Nattrass* [1971] 2 All ER 127 where the House of Lords held that a local branch manager was 'another person' whose act or default could result in the commission of the relevant offence since that manager could not be regarded as part of the controlling mind and will of the company. That principle was clarified in *R v Boal* [1992] 1 QB 591, a case concerning the Fire Precautions Act 1971, where it was held that a 'manager' was someone who had the power and responsibility to decide company policy and strategy.

Due diligence
'Where Parliament in creating an offence of "strict liability" has also provided that it shall be a defence if the person on whom the duty is imposed proves that *he* exercised all due diligence to avoid a breach of the duty, the clear intention of Parliament is to mitigate the injustice, which may be involved in an offence of strict liability, of subjecting to punishment a careful and conscientious person who is in no way to blame' (*Tesco Supermarkets Ltd v Nattrass* [1971] 2 All ER 127, *per* Lord Diplock, p 158e).

The only defence under the FSA is that of due diligence the purpose of which is to avoid conviction of a defendant who did all he reasonably could to prevent breach of the law. The defence, which is new to food law, is contained in s 21 of the FSA. However, it is not entirely new as it arises in a number of other important consumer protection statutes, such as the Trade Descriptions Act 1968 and Consumer Protection Act 1987.

Section 21(1) states that it is a defence for the person charged to prove that he took all reasonable precautions and exercised all due diligence to avoid the commission of the offence by him or by a person under his control.

The offences to which s 21 relate are those in the 'preceding provisions' of Pt II of the Act, that is, the offences created by ss 7, 8, 14 and 15 of the FSA and, technically, to the offences of breaching an order or notice served on the proprietor of a food business.

Part II of the FSA contains the power of ministers to make regulations (s 16). Section 49 of the FSA empowers ministers to apply various provisions, including the provisions of the FSA to those regulations. Section 21 has been applied to the Food Safety (General Food Hygiene) Regulations 1995 and the Food Safety (Temperature Control) Regulations 1995, as well as other regulations which govern hygiene in specific industries.

The burden of proof is on the person charged to prove the defence (*Amos v Melcon (Frozen Foods) Ltd* (1985) 149 JP 712) to the civil standard of proof, that is, on the balance of probabilities. However, there are three reasons why enforcement officers should, when investigating an alleged offence, also consider whether the prospective defendant may have a defence under s 21. First, *Code of Practice No 2: Legal Matters* recommends that, before deciding to prosecute, food authorities should consider, *inter alia*, 'the likelihood of the defendant being able to establish a due diligence defence'. Secondly, by investigating whether a due diligence defence is available, the enforcement officer may establish that the offence was caused by the act or default of a third party in which case the by-pass provisions of s 20 (see above) can be invoked to prosecute that other person. Thirdly, enforcement officers are obliged to caution a prospective defendant where they establish sufficient evidence on which to found a charge. Lack of a due diligence system relevant to the alleged offence may provide that 'sufficient evidence'.

The person charged must demonstrate a causal link between the offence for which he was charged and that part of his due diligence system which specifically relates to the charge. There is no requirement to prove that every part of the due diligence system was operating effectively at the time the offence is committed. Section 21(1) states that '[i]n any proceedings for *an offence* . . . it shall be a defence . . . to prove that he took all reasonable precautions and all due diligence to avoid the commission of *the offence* . . .'. Any attempt by the prosecution to put before the court deficiencies in the overall system which are irrelevant to the charge should be challenged on the grounds that they are prejudicial and inadmissible.

Section 21 distinguishes between three broad categories of person who can avail themselves of the defence, the person who prepared or imported the food into Great Britain, the own labeller and the person selling branded goods. The section provides that the preparer and importer of food must establish what can be called the 'full' due diligence defence, that is, all the constituent elements of s 21(1). In the case of offences under ss 8, 14 and 15, the own labeller and the person selling branded goods are entitled to rely on a lesser form of due diligence defence set out in ss 21(3) and (4), the so-called 'deemed' due diligence defence.

The preparer or importer of food

The identity of the 'preparer of food' is not prescribed by s 21 of the FSA. However, 'preparation' is defined in s 53 as 'including manufacture and any form of processing or treatment'. 'Treatment' is defined in s 53 as 'includ[ing] subjecting [food] to heat or cold'. It is clear from these definitions that a manufacturer or caterer is a 'preparer of food'. What is less obvious is that, in certain circumstances, a retailer can be a person who prepares food. Many retailers will stock food which is 'subject[ed] to cold' by virtue of storing chilled or frozen food in refrigeration equipment. If that is the case, the retailer will have to establish the full due diligence defence notwithstanding that, in the ordinary sense of the word, he did not 'prepare' the food. It is submitted that this analysis affords the public maximum protection as the onus rests on the retailer to have in place proper systems to ensure that refrigeration equipment used by him functions properly and is monitored regularly.

'Importation' has the same meaning ascribed to it in the Customs and Excise Management Act 1979 (s 53). The definition of 'importer' in s 1(1) of that Act includes the legal owner, the person beneficially interested in the goods and the person in possession of the goods during the period between importation and delivery.

The own labeller

A person charged with an offence under s 8, 14 or 15 above who neither prepared nor imported into Great Britain the food is deemed to establish the due diligence defence if he proves three distinct requirements set out in s 21(3):

(1) that the offence was caused by the act or default of another person who was not under his control, or to reliance on information supplied by that person;

(2) that he carried out all such checks of the food in question as were reasonable in all the circumstances, or that it was reasonable in all the circumstances for him to rely on checks carried out by the person who supplied the food to him; and

(3) that he did not know and had no reason to suspect at the time of the commission of the alleged offence that his act or omission would amount to an offence under the relevant provision.

The seller of branded goods

A person charged with an offence under s 8, 14 or 15 of the FSA who neither prepared nor imported the food must also establish three facts in order to be deemed to have established the deemed due diligence defence set out in s 21(4):

(1) that the offence was caused by the act or default of another person who was not under his control, or to reliance on information supplied by that person;

(2) that the sale or intended sale was not one under his 'name or mark' and

(3) that the person selling the goods did not know, and could not reasonably have been expected to know at the time the offence was committed that his act or omission would amount to an offence under the relevant provision of the FSA.

Sections 21(3)(a) and 21(4)(a) are identical. 'Act or default' means wrongful act or default. It must be proved that the third party committed that wrongful act or default. The phrase 'another person who was not under his control' is important. 'Another person' in s 20 could be an employee of a company charged with the offence if that employee cannot be regarded as being part of the controlling mind or will of the company (*Tesco Supermarkets Ltd v Nattrass* [1971] 2 All ER 127). However, the addition of the words, 'who was not under his control' takes out of the scope of s 21(3)(a) and 21(4)(a) the employee since he necessarily would be someone over whom the company charged had control (except possibly where the employee was acting entirely outside the scope of his employment). Increasingly, larger food businesses engage food safety consultants to advise them on their legal obligations and to devise due diligence systems rather than employing in-house qualified environmental health officers. It is submitted that the former will not be under the business's control where the contractual relationship is one of independent contractor and employer.

Whether the third party is under the control of the person charged is a question of fact. A person who on the face of it appears to be independent of the person charged may be controlled by the person charged. For example, where a food retailer has a subsidiary company which supplies food to it, it is likely that the court will require evidence that the two companies are operated as separate entities. Companies selling own label products, particularly the major multiples, have close relationships with their suppliers, providing them with detailed product specifications and, frequently, production requirements. It is submitted that these facts are insufficient to constitute the requisite degree of control envisaged by s 21 but, rather they are factors in an overall due diligence system to be expected of businesses of that nature, size and resources.

The wording of s 21(3)(c) reflects the fact that, because of the requirements of s 21(3)(b), the own labeller needs to have a greater understanding of his supplier's systems in order to establish 'reasonable' reliance on the supplier. Accordingly, s 21(3)(c) places a higher evidential burden on the own labeller to show that he did not know and had no reason to suspect that an offence was being committed. The person selling branded goods, however, is likely to have a far more arms length relationship with his supplier and less knowledge of his due diligence systems and so only needs to prove that he did not know, and could not reasonably have been expected to know, that an offence was being committed.

The notice requirements of section 21

One of the problems prosecutors have is that they may only learn of a defence at the last minute, leaving little or no time to consider its merits in order to assess whether the prosecution should proceed. A procedural requirement incorporated into s 21 militates against this as s 21(5) requires defendants who wish to rely on a due diligence defence to serve on the prosecutor at least seven clear days before the hearing and, where the defendant has previously appeared before the court in connection with the alleged offence, within one month of that appearance (defined in s 21(6) as including being brought before a court), a written notice identifying or assisting in the identification of the third party whose act or default is alleged to have resulted in the commission of the offence or on whose information he relied.

There is no prescribed form for the notice. Service on the prosecution must comply with the requirements of s 50(1)(b) that is, it must either be left at or posted to the office of the prosecutor.

Section 21(5) refers to the notice being served where it is alleged that 'another person' caused the offence to be committed. The due diligence defence relates to the acts of a third party and not someone who is under the control of the person charged, for example, an employee (see s 21(1)). In theory, therefore, it appears that s 21(5) does not require service of a notice where the person charged alleges that the act or default was that of his employee. However, since the mischief that the section is intended to address is to prevent the prosecution being taken by surprise by a due diligence defence, it is submitted that a notice should be served irrespective of the identity of the third party. Possibly, the prosecution may decide after receipt of the notice to use the by-pass provisions of s 20 to charge that other person for the offence and to withdraw the summons against the person originally charged.

The due diligence defence can be relied on where a notice is not served or is served out of time where the court gives leave to do so.

It is preferable, however, to ensure that the notice is served on time rather than relying on the discretion of the court to allow submission of the defence.

The meaning of 'due diligence'

No definition is given in the FSA of what is meant by 'all reasonable precautions and all due diligence'. Those words appear in other consumer protection legislation and have been and continue to be considered by the courts. Although some general principles can be extracted from this case law, it must be remembered that the meaning of the words is a question of fact to be decided in each individual case so care should be taken to analyse facts in detail rather than relying exclusively on legal precedent.

The defence has two elements. To 'take reasonable precautions' is to be able to prove that a system of control exists which will contemplate all foreseeable problems and deal with them. The system should be able to highlight situations which could lead to offences being committed. It should provide mechanisms for responding to the difficulty highlighted. The second element, due diligence, will be established if the company is able to prove that the system was in fact operating effectively.

Some general principles can be extracted from the leading cases on the meaning of 'due diligence'. Where the person charged is a limited company a failure to exercise due diligence on its part would only occur where the failure was that of a director or senior manager in actual control of the company's operations who could be identified with the controlling mind and will of the company. It is consistent with the taking of reasonable precautions and the exercise of due diligence to institute an effective system to avoid the offence being committed under which superior servants are instructed to supervise inferior servants whose acts might lead to the commission of the offence; this is not the delegation of the duty to exercise due diligence but the performance of that duty (*Tesco Supermarkets Ltd v Nattrass* [1971] 2 All ER 127).

Where delegation of a function or part of a function takes place, the outcome or end result may differ or vary according to the nature of the offence created by the statute. Statutes are principally of two kinds: first, those creating strict liability and, secondly, those where liability is based on criminal intent. The FSA is a statute which creates offences of strict liability for which there is a defence of due diligence so long as commission of the relevant offence was not referable to neglect. 'Due diligence is in law the converse of negligence and negligence connotes a reprehensible state of mind – a lack of care for the consequences of his physical acts on the part of the person doing them' (*Tesco Supermarkets Ltd v Nattrass*, per Lord Diplock, p155). The process of delegating functions and responsibilities normally transfers liability from the organisation to the person to whom performance of the statutory duty was delegated. Where it is established that no neglect or fault lies with the director who delegated the duty, the individual to whom it was delegated, namely the other person, may well be liable.

'All reasonable precautions' must be taken and what is reasonable depends on the nature and size of the relevant business. In *Bibby-Cheshire v Golden Wonder Ltd* [1972] 3 All ER 738, the Divisional Court accepted that no machine existed which was accurate enough to eliminate all under-weight crisp packets and that it was not economically viable for a company even of the size of Golden Wonder individually to weigh each of the 20 million packets it produced. In *Garratt v Boots The Chemists Ltd*, (16 July 1980 unreported), Lord Lane said 'what might be reasonable for a large retailer might not be reasonable for the village shop'. The court held that Boots did not take all reasonable precautions to avoid selling pencils containing excess lead because a reasonable precaution which could have been taken was to institute a system of random sampling. If a sampling system is used, it must be sufficient for the purpose for which it was designed; there must be statistical evidence as to the amount of product it is reasonable to test to avoid faults, the test results must be communicated to the business and acted on (*P & M Supplies (Essex) Ltd v Devon County Council* (1992) 156 JP 328 where only 0.5 per cent of toys imported from China were tested for defects; see also *L B Sutton v David Halsall plc* (1995) 159 JP 431; cf *Hurley v Martinez & Co Ltd* [1991] CCLR 1, where the Divisional Court upheld the acquittal of a small wine retailer who argued a due diligence defence under the Trade Descriptions Act 1968 in respect of a charge of selling mislabelled wine incorrectly stating alcoholic strength. The error happened at the West German winery regulated by the West German Government through sampling by state laboratories. The results of those tests were not disclosed to the retailer and he had no independent system of sampling products. Instead he relied on assurances of his suppliers).

It is not sufficient to obtain from suppliers a general warranty or assurance that goods supplied comply with all relevant laws; the warranty must relate to specific goods supplied (*Riley v Webb* (1987) 151 JP 372).

Codes of practice, industry guides and internal guidance can give the court some guidance on the standard expected of the defendant but they are not sufficient in themselves to prove compliance with the law. Similarly, proof of compliance with a British Standard is not enough; the business must have taken steps to avoid falling below the standard set by the law (*Balding v Lew Ways Ltd* (1995) *The Times*, 9 March where a toy complied with a British Standard but not the requirements of the Toys (Safety) Regulations 1989 (SI No 1275) and the Consumer Protection Act 1987).

The defence is not available where the employer does not properly select, train and supervise staff in order that they are competent to carry out the relevant task (*Knowsley Metropolitan Borough Council v Cowan* (1992) 156 JP 45, DC). Instructions to staff must be sufficient so that they can perform their duties (*Turtington v United Co-operatives* [1993] Crim LR 376).

The fact that a trading standards department was opposite the premises of a toy importer who had invited them to take samples which they had done was insufficient to establish that all reasonable precautions had been taken to avoid supplying a toy which had too high a lead content (*Taylor v Lawrence Fraser (Bristol) Ltd* (1977) 121 SJ 757). However, in *Carrick District Council v Taunton Vale Meat Traders Ltd* (1994) 158 JP 347, the Divisional Court held that meat traders could show that they took all reasonable precautions and exercised all due diligence where they relied, as an essential part of their system, upon a meat inspector's certificate certifying beef as fit for human consumption when in fact it was unfit. There was nothing in the words of s 21(1) which prevented a defendant from relying upon the action of a third party in his attempt to show that he had taken all reasonable precautions and exercised all due diligence. The prosecution had argued that the meat traders had to take positive action themselves by setting up their own system for checking the meat and supervising the system to ensure it worked. They had submitted that if it were possible to take any precaution, which had not been taken, due diligence had not been exercised. In rejecting that submission, Smith J said, '. . . that proposition is too wide as the statutory defence calls for all "reasonable precautions" and all "due diligence", rather than all "possible precautions" and all "possible diligence".

The principle in civil law of *res ipsa loquitur* has no application to s 21 of the FSA. In *Cow & Gate Limited v Westminster City Council* (14 March 1995, unreported), the company was charged with selling to the prejudice of the purchaser a jar of baby food which was not of the substance demanded as it contained a piece of bone, contrary to s 14 of the FSA. Although the magistrate found that the company had taken all reasonable precautions by designing a system to avoid foreign bodies entering or escaping through the system, he convicted the company, drawing the inference that they had not exercised all due diligence simply because of the presence of the bone in the jar. The Divisional Court held that the magistrate had made an error of law and quashed the conviction. '. . . [T]he presence of the bone . . . create[d] the offence under s 14. If it were also to negative the defence under s 21, that section would be wholly devoid of effect.' (*per* Balcombe LJ).

Proving all due diligence

Although it is not a legal requirement to have formally documented management procedures aimed at ensuring compliance with the FSA and subordinate regulations, in practice it is likely to be much more difficult to establish the due diligence defence to the satisfaction of a court without documentation. Secondly, it is necessary to show clear-cut evidence of the implementation of management procedures. In all too many cases, procedures have been established but were disregarded or, alternatively, people had not received the appropriate training and management supervision to ensure satisfactory operation of them.

Codes of recommended practice

Section 40 of the FSA empowers ministers (Ministry of Agriculture, Fisheries and Food, Department of Health, Scottish Office and Welsh Office) to issue codes of recommended practice as regards the execution and enforcement of the Act and of regulations and orders made under it. Food authorities are required to have regard to any relevant provision of any such code.

In the case of alleged breaches of the FSGFHR, reference should be made to statutory Code of Practice No 9 *Food Hygiene Inspections* (revised September 1995) which gives guidance to food authorities on the frequency and nature of inspections carried out to assess the hygiene of premises and the public health protection aspects of food law. Annex A to this code contains advice on a scheme to assess the potential risk posed by food businesses and guidance on the frequency of inspection. Other statutory codes which may be of significance in the preparation of a defence are statutory codes No 2 *Legal Matters* and No 3 *Inspection Procedures – General. Guidelines on the Statutory Defence of Due Diligence* have also been issued jointly by the Chartered Institute of Environmental Health, the Food & Drink Federation, the Local Authorities Co-ordinating body on food and Trading Standards (LACOTS), the National Consumer Council, the National Farmers Union and the Retail Consortium.

Management systems and procedures

As with the majority of consumer protection legislation nowadays, the principal emphasis of the FSA and regulations made under the Act is on the development and implementation of management systems aimed at the prevention of incidents or situations which could result in injury, damage or loss.

So what are the management systems that must be established to be able to prove 'all reasonable precautions and all due diligence' on behalf of a client? The control systems must cover all aspects of the operation of the business which concern compliance with legal requirements. Moreover, these control systems must be subject to regular review and amendment as necessary. The various control systems are outlined below.

Hazard analysis and quality assurance
There is a need critically to examine the nature of the business to identify areas of risk which should be subject to appropriate controls. This implies use of the quality technique known as Hazard Analysis: Critical Control Points (HACCP) which has been introduced into many major food companies over the last decade. This technique entails the identification of food hazards arising at certain points in a process (the critical control points), the measurement and evaluation of the risks arising from these hazards, specification of the various controls necessary (temperature, bacteriological quality, etc.) and the monitoring systems to meet these specifications. (The HACCP technique is described in detail in Chapter 9.)

Statement of policy on food safety (mission statement)
Whilst there is no legal requirement for a formal written policy, as with a statement of health and safety policy, such a document has

value in setting out the objectives, organisation, arrangements and individual responsibilities for ensuring food safety and legal compliance. Many organisations operate such policies as part of their management procedures.

Cleaning and planned preventive maintenance
Chapter I of Sched 1, Rules of Hygiene, FSGFHR states that food premises must be kept clean and maintained in good repair and condition.

A formal cleaning schedule or programme should indicate each item or area for cleaning, the methods, materials and equipment to be used, the frequency of cleaning and individual management responsibilities. Similarly, planned preventive maintenance systems should formally indicate each item of plant and equipment to be maintained, perhaps by reference to a plant register, the maintenance procedure, frequency of maintenance and individual responsibility for ensuring the procedures are implemented.

Temperature control arrangements
Well-established procedures, together with the necessary instrumentation to provide information on temperature controls, must be in operation, including procedures to be followed by operators where there are deviations from the temperature control requirements of the Food Safety (Temperature Control) Regulations 1995.

Infestation control systems
A formally documented infestation control system, which ensures the identification of any form of infestation by rodents, crawling and flying insects and birds at an early stage of that infestation, must be operated. Where an organisation uses the services of a commercial pest control company, evidence of monitoring of the performance of that company to ensure contract compliance must be available.

Training and supervision
Chapter X of Sched 1, Rules of Hygiene, FSGFHR places an absolute duty on the proprietor of a food business to ensure that food handlers engaged in the food business are supervised and instructed and/or trained in food hygiene matters commensurate with their work activity. Written procedures indicating the nature, extent and content of the training, the groups of trainees involved and the results of such training should be maintained.

Precautions and checks
The availability and use of food safety manuals, internal codes of practice and operating instructions is an important feature of proving due diligence. Furthermore, internal inspection procedures, whether by scheduled or unscheduled inspections, should show evidence of remedying any deficiencies promptly and efficiently. Such inspections should incorporate a number of features, in particular an examination and assessment of the hygiene routines of staff, structural state and cleanliness, layout of food production and storage areas, state of plant, machinery and equipment, environmental factors, such as lighting, maintenance of cleaning and housekeeping procedures, infestation prevention and control procedures, and control over raw materials and ingredients.

Corrective action
As with any quality system, the system must be capable of detecting faults and indicating the corrective action necessary where appropriate.

Consumer complaints
Consumer complaints must be taken seriously, recorded, analysed and acted upon in order to detect possible faults in the system. A formal written product recall procedure should also be available and operated in extreme situations.

Procedures following enforcement action
There should be a formal procedure for taking action in the event of the service of an improvement notice or emergency prohibition notice by the food authority and/or where a court may make a prohibition order or emergency prohibition order.

Liaison with food authority officers
Procedures for liaison with the food authority and its officers are vital. A senior manager should be delegated to deal with all complaints and to meet with enforcement officers where appropriate.

Health surveillance
Internal health surveillance procedures, such as the systems for pre-employment health screening, health examinations of staff on return to work following sickness and other methods to ensure

freedom from infection transmittable to food, should be documented along with evidence of their implementation.

Documentation of procedures, systems, policies and instructions is the key factor, together with clearly demonstrated evidence of the implementation and management of the system. Evidence of staff training in their individual responsibilities, hygiene and cleaning procedures, and in techniques like HACCP is also important if an 'all due diligence' defence is to be established.

Publication in the course of a business

Section 15 of the FSA creates the offence of falsely describing or presenting food with regard to labels which may falsely describe the food or mislead as to the nature or the substance or quality of a particular food (see Chapter 3).

There is a specific statutory defence to s 15 contained in s 22 of the FSA which is new to food safety law but which corresponds to that provided in s 25 of the Trade Descriptions Act 1968. The defence is aimed at protecting an individual who, on a *bona fide* basis, has published material, such as a label, or an advertisement, which is illegal.

In order to establish the defence, an advertiser must prove two facts:

(a) that he is in the business of publishing or arranging the publication of advertisements; and

(b) that he received the advertisement in the ordinary course of his business and that he did not know and had no reason to suspect that its publication would amount to an offence.

The burden of proof is on the advertiser to prove the statutory defence on the balance of probabilities. Like the seller of branded goods who relies on the deemed due diligence defence in s 21(4) of the FSA, the advertiser only has to prove that he, 'had no reason to suspect' that an offence was being committed rather than the higher standard of proof required for the own labeller under s 21(3) that he could not reasonably be expected to know that the offence was being committed. It is submitted that the lesser standard reflects the fact that, unlike the own labeller, the advertiser is unlikely to have any input into the formulation of advertisements submitted to him for publication and therefore would not be in a position to know what procedures, if any, his customer had to avoid the commission of an offence under s 15.

Chapter 6

Administration and Enforcement

Introduction

The FSA is administered and enforced by both central and local government. The Department of Health and the Ministry of Agriculture, Fisheries and Food are the responsible government departments in England and Wales. The Secretary of State (Scottish Office) exercises similar powers in Scotland. At local government level, the Act and regulations are enforced by the various food authorities, the general and specific duties of which are outlined below.

Enforcement by central government

Responsible government departments

Under s 4 of the FSA the 'Minister' is defined in England and Wales, as the Minister of Agriculture, Fisheries and Food or the Secretary of State for Health, and in Scotland, the Secretary of State for Scotland. The expression 'Ministers' means in England the Minister of Agriculture, Fisheries and Food and the Secretary of State for Health acting jointly, and in Wales the Minister of Agriculture, Fisheries and Food and the Secretary for Wales also acting jointly. The Minister of Agriculture, Fisheries and Food or the Secretary of State for Scotland may make emergency control orders under s 13 of the FSA (s 4(2)).

Power to make regulations

The Ministers are given wide-ranging powers to make regulations. Full details of these powers are to be found in s 16 as amplified in Sched 1 of the FSA.

The principal regulation-making power in s 16 enables regulations to be made to cover:

(a) food composition both generally and as to specific substances;

(b) food safety including microbiological standards;

(c) food processing and treatment;

(d) food hygiene;

(e) labelling, marketing, presenting or advertising food; and

(f) any other matter as to food or food sources which is necessary or expedient in the interests of public health or consumer protection.

Schedule 1 expands on (a) to (d) above as well as making provision for regulations to ensure inspection of food sources by authorised officers of enforcement authorities. 'Food sources' are defined in s 1(3) of the FSA and mean any growing crop or live animal, bird or fish from which food is intended to be derived.

Regulations may also be made under s 16(2) as regards food contact materials, ie any article or substance which is intended to come into contact with food.

A further regulation-making power is to be found in s 17 of the FSA for the implementation of any EU obligations. The regulations to implement Council Directive 93/43/EEC (the Hygiene of Foodstuffs Directive) have been implemented under this (as well as other) regulation-making powers. Regulations may also be made to provide sanctions etc for directly applicable EU provisions (ie EU regulations).

The power of the ministers to make regulations under s 16 enables the government to respond, in particular, to advances in food technology, eg the irradiation of foodstuffs and novel foods.

Irradiated foods

The Food (Control of Irradiation) Regulations 1990 (SI 1990 No 2490) authorise the irradiation of food in the UK, subject to strict licensing controls on treatment facilities, and the use of such 'properly irradiated food' (defined in reg 2(2) of the regulations). The licensing system is administered by central government. It is permitted only to irradiate seven types of foodstuffs – fruit, vegetables, cereals, bulbs and tubers, spices and condiments, fish and shellfish and poultry (reg 2(2)(c) and (d)). Only one licence has, to date, been issued; this is for the irradiation of spices as irradiation is considered a safer option than the previously used method of treatment.

The requirements of food labelling for irradiated food are contained in sections 26A, 28(3A), 29(2) and (4A), 29(5) and 33(1) [1A–1D] of the Food Labelling Regulations 1984 which were added/substituted by the Food Labelling Amendment (Irradiated Foods) Regulations 1990. These regulations implemented Council Directive (EEC) 89/395 in respect of the labelling of irradiated food. Both pre-packed and non-prepacked food which is exposed for sale must be marked or labelled either that it or an ingredient of it has been irradiated, with the word 'irradiated' or the words 'treated with ionising irradiation'. Where such food is sold in a catering establishment to the ultimate consumer, the relevant words must appear on the label or on a menu, notice, ticket or label that is readily discernible by an intending purchaser at the place where he chooses the food (eg the self-service counter, delicatessen counter, at the table in the restaurant): reg 33(1A). Caterers who sell irradiated food to the ultimate consumer are permitted to say on the menu, for example, that the food 'may' contain irradiated ingredients (reg 33(1B), (1C) and (1D)). Food sold to caterers which has been irradiated or which contains irradiated ingredients must be labelled either on the label attached to the food or on a ticket or notice displayed in immediate proximity to the food or in relevant trade documents furnished on or before delivery of the food (reg 33(2)).

Novel foods and genetically modified food sources

Novel food is any food which has not previously been used for human consumption in Great Britain or has only been used to a very limited extent: s 18(3). A genetically modified food source is one in which any genes or genetic material has been artificially modified or is otherwise derived or inherited by replication from modified genetic material. Selective breeding techniques and *in vitro* fertilisation are not regarded as artificial for these purposes (s 18(4)).

Section 18(1) gives ministers a specific power to deal with novel foods rather than such foods being controlled under s 16. Section

18(1) enables the ministers to make regulations to cover three particular types of food:

(i)   novel foods, including novel food sources;
(ii) genetically modified food sources or foods derived from such sources; and
(iii) imported food.

The regulations may impose appropriate prohibitions on such foods or food sources subject to specified exceptions including in the case of imported food allowing importation via authorised places of entry such as named ports or aerodromes.

Enforcement by local government

Local enforcement is undertaken by the various food authorities and their authorised officers (ss 5 and 6).

In England and Wales these are councils of London boroughs, districts or non-metropolitan counties; the Common Council of the City of London; and the appropriate Treasurer of the Inner or Middle Temple (s 5(1)).

The food authorities in Scotland are the islands or district councils (s 5(2)).

The duties of food authorities may be placed upon a port health authority or (in Scotland) a port local authority, a joint board or a unitary authority created under the Local Government Act 1985. Where this happens, references in the FSA to a food authority are taken to be references to such an authority or board (s 5(3)).

The ministers may order that any functions under this Act which are exercisable concurrently by more than one authority must be exercisable solely by one specified authority (s 5(4)).

The relevant officers and authorities are defined in s 5(5).

Authorised officers

An authorised officer, in relation to a food authority, means any person (whether or not an officer of the authority) who is authorised by them in writing, either generally or specifically, to act in matters arising under the FSA. However, ministers may regulate that no person shall be authorised unless he has certain prescribed qualifications (s 5(6)).

A food authority may authorise a variety of officers to act on its behalf, eg environmental health officers, sampling officers, meat inspectors and other specialists. An authorised officer must be authorised in writing by the food authority.

The importance of ss 5(6) and 6(6) is that they empower the ministers to prescribe qualifications for authorised officers. The training, qualifications and appointment of authorised officers are currently being reviewed.

Enforcement of the Act

Section 6(2) places a general duty on food authorities to enforce and execute the provisions of the FSA for all purposes except where a duty is expressly or by necessary implication placed upon another authority. In certain cases, subs (5) empowers the minister or ministers to take over the conduct of proceedings which have been instituted by some other person.

The ministers may direct, in relation to cases of a particular description or in a particular case, that any duty imposed on food authorities by subs (2) above must be discharged by the ministers or the minister and not by those authorities (s 6(3)).

Regulations or orders under the FSA must specify which of the following authorities are to enforce and execute them, either generally or in relation to cases of a particular description or a particular area namely:

(a) the ministers, the minister, food authorities or other authorities mentioned in s 5(3) above; and

(b) in the case of regulations, the Commissioners of Customs and Excise.

Any such regulations or orders may provide for any authorised authority to inform and assist another (s 6(4)).

Division of responsibilities

The functions to be exercised by district and county councils are detailed in *Code of Practice No 1: Responsibility for the Enforcement of the Food Safety Act 1990.* This division of responsibilities is similar to the former division of activities between the environmental health departments of district councils and the trading standards departments run by county councils. The code does not affect the London boroughs or the metropolitan areas where there are single tier authorities, port health authorities which carry out the full range of functions, or Scotland, where all enforcement is carried out at district level.

Co-ordinating groups

Code of Practice No 1 emphasises the need for effective liaison between district and county councils. It advises that food authorities which do not already have liaison arrangements should set up a co-ordinating group between the officers of the county council, those of the districts within that county and, where appropriate, the port health authorities within that county. Liaison should involve authorised officers, public analysts, food examiners and any other experts needed to advise the authorities on special issues. It may also involve, from time to time, officers of the State Veterinary Service.

The co-ordinating group's functions should include:
(a) making arrangements for programmed inspections, especially in food manufacturing premises;
(b) arranging for co-ordinated advice on specific topics to be provided to businesses in the area;
(c) arranging for the transfer of any complaint and the associated sample of food where that has been received at the offices of one food authority but is in fact the responsibility of another;
(d) supplying information on the names and telephone numbers of individuals dealing with food law in their authority to any other food authorities covering the same area;
(e) providing a channel for the resolution of any difficulties which may arise;
(f) co-ordinating sampling programmes;
(g) recommending priorities for enforcement action; and
(h) co-ordination on taking legal proceedings.

The code further recommends that each county and district council should also designate a specific liaison officer and, where possible, a deputy. The liaison officer should act as the first point of contact for those in all other food authorities, not only those covered by the co-ordinating group.

Enquiries and complaints

Any food authority approached by a member of the public seeking advice under the FSA or making a complaint should provide all the assistance it can. The food authority should not suggest to an individual seeking advice or making a complaint that he or she should travel to the offices of another enforcement authority. The county or district concerned should agree arrangements for transferring details of the complaint and/or samples of food where this is necessary.

Division of enforcement arrangements

Whilst both county councils and district councils may take legal proceedings under ss 7, 8 and 14 of the FSA, responsibility should be divided as follows:

District councils
    (a) contamination of food by micro-organisms or their toxins, such as salmonella, listeria or botulism;
    (b) chemical contamination situations which pose an imminent risk to health;
    (c) contamination by mould or foreign matter found in food.

County councils
    (a) contamination by chemicals and improper use of additives;
    (b) compositional offences;
    (c) adulteration of food; and
    (d) misleading claims related to food.

Section 15, which deals with falsely describing or presenting food, is, however, purely a trading standards matter and so in non-metropolitan counties the county council will be the enforcement authority.

The code also emphasises that, where malicious tampering with food is suspected, the food authority should contact the police. The subject of malicious tampering is dealt with in *Code of Practice No 16: Enforcement of the Food Safety Act 1990 in Relation to the Food Hazard Warning System*. (See Chapter 8, p 149.)

Administrators

Sections 27 and 28 of the FSA are concerned with the appointment, qualifications and remuneration of public analysts and the provision of facilities for examinations respectively.

Appointment of public analysts

Every food authority in England and Wales and every regional or islands council in Scotland must appoint one or more persons (in the FSA referred to as public analysts) to act as analysts for the purposes of the Act within the authority's area.

Anyone appointed as a public analyst must possess the necessary qualifications as prescribed in regulations or approved by the ministers.

The Food Safety (Sampling and Qualifications) Regulations 1990 (SI 1990 No 2463) lay down qualifications for both food analysts and food examiners. A food analyst means a public analyst or other person qualified to carry out analyses. A food examiner is a person qualified to carry out microbiological examinations. These regulations also prescribe the form of certificate to be given by food analysts and food examiners when they have dealt with samples submitted to them. (See Appendix 2.)

No person must act as a public analyst for any area if he is engaged directly or indirectly in any food business which is carried on in that area (s 27(2)).

A failure by a food authority to comply with the requirements of the above regulations with regard to the qualifications of a food analyst or examiner could form the basis for a legal challenge of an alleged breach of ss 7, 8 and 14 of the Act.

Remuneration of public analysts

Section 27(3) provides for remuneration of a public analyst as may be agreed and the circumstances and conditions under which the remuneration may be paid.

Appointment of deputy public analysts

Section 27(4) empowers an authority to whom this section applies which appoints only one public analyst to appoint a deputy to act during any vacancy in the office of the public analyst, or during his absence or incapacity. The terms and conditions of his appointment are the same as those outlined above for the public analyst and any statutory references are deemed to include references to the deputy.

For the purposes of s 27(1) above 'food authority' does not include the council of a non-metropolitan district, the Sub-Treasurer of the Inner Temple or the Under-Treasurer of the Middle Temple; and in s 27(2) the reference to being engaged directly or indirectly in a food business includes a reference to having made such arrangements with a food business as may be prescribed by regulations made by the ministers. To date, no regulations specifically provide for such arrangements to be made but the Food Safety (Sampling and Qualifications) Regulations 1990 provide that no director, owner or employee of a food business, or partner in a food business, shall act as a public analyst for the area in which the business is situated (reg 5(1)).

Provision of facilities for examinations

Food authorities in England and Wales and regional councils in Scotland have a discretionary power to provide facilities for the examination of food (s 28(1)). Examination means a microbiological examination (s 28(2)).

Analysis and examination

The distinction between analysis and examination is important. Analysis is defined in s 53 as including microbiological assay and any technique for establishing the composition of food. These techniques include, for instance, testing on the basis of smell, taste, appearance and texture, ingredient specification, the presence or otherwise of foreign material, and conformance to a legal standard. Microbiological assay could include an ongoing bacteriological sampling programme, conducted over a period of time, directed at all the stages of a food manufacturing process to assess the effectiveness of a cleaning programme. Examination, however, means a microbiological examination (s 28(2)). This implies the taking of a sample and an examination of that sample to detect the presence or otherwise of pathogenic and other harmful organisms.

The public analyst and the Public Health Laboratory Service

The public analyst has an important role in providing an analytical service of the composition of food and water, and for detecting the presence of a range of contaminants, such as metals, taints, pesticides, chemical pollutants and additives. The public analyst also provides an advisory service to the food authority and individual authorised officers with regard to samples and sampling procedures for certain types and classes of food.

The Public Health Laboratory Service (PHLS) was initially established under the National Health Service Acts to provide a surveillance and control service in connection with infectious diseases in England and Wales. There are a number of regional laboratories, together with the Communicable Disease Surveillance Centre, located at Colindale.

One of the principal functions of the PHLS is that of providing microbiological expertise to authorised officers from environmental health departments in the investigation of food poisoning incidents. This may entail the examination of faecal specimens, water and suspect foods in an attempt to identify and isolate pathogens causing illness. The PHLS also undertakes routine examination of water and a wide range of food samples.

Non-government organisations

Local Authorities Co-ordinating Body on Food and Trading Standards (LACOTS)

LACOTS has played a significant role in achieving consistency of interpretation and enforcement of the FSA by food authorities. It provides guidance on many issues and co-operates with other official bodies, such as the Department of Health, Ministry of Agriculture, Fisheries and Food, National Consumer Council, the Chartered Institute of Environmental Health, the Food and Drink Federation, the National Farmers Union and the Retail Consortium. Their joint publication *Food Safety Act 1990: Guidelines on the Statutory Defence of Due Diligence* is an example of such guidance, together with LACOTS' own publications, *Guidance on Food Hygiene Inspections: General guidance notes to assist local authorities undertaking programmed food hygiene inspections (June 1993)* and *Guidance on Food Complaints: Guidance for dealing with food complaints made to local environmental health departments (January 1994)*. Whilst the advice provided by LACOTS in its various publications has no legal status, compliance may be seen as evidence of best practice by authorised officers and proprietors of food businesses. The role of LACOTS was extended to include food hygiene co-ordination in 1992.

Other advisory committees and groups

There are a number of non-government organisations who provide advisory services to the ministers. These include the Advisory Committee on Pesticides, the Veterinary Products Committee, the Committee on the Microbiological Safety of Food, the Steering

Group on Food Surveillance, the Advisory Committee on Novel Foods and Processes, the Committee on Toxicity of Chemicals in Food, Consumer Protection and the Environment and the Committee on the Carcinogenicity of Chemicals in Food, Consumer Protection and the Environment.

Food Advisory Committee

The government's Food Advisory Committee comprises a range of people, eg technologists, civil servants and lawyers. They advise the ministers on a variety of issues relating to food safety, such as composition, quality, bacteriological and other standards.

The Committee also has the function of advising the minister of the need for new or modified food safety legislation, the interpretation and implementation of European Directives and on measures for promoting food safety practices throughout the United Kingdom.

Registration of food premises

Under s 19 of the FSA, the ministers may make regulations for the registration of food premises and the licensing of premises, either to secure compliance with food safety requirements, or in the interest of public health or protecting the interests of consumers. Regulations covering registration made in 1991 are in effect but no regulations relating to licensing have yet been produced.

The Food Premises (Registration) Regulations 1991 (SI 1991 No 2825)

With certain exceptions, these regulations provide for the registration of all food premises and make it an offence to carry on a food business from unregistered premises. The main purpose of registration is to provide food authorities with information about food businesses within their area, so they can target inspection, sampling and enforcement resources more effectively.

The obligation to register, and to notify changes in the nature of the food business, rests with the proprietor of the food business (reg 4), or the person who permits the use of premises where such premises are used by more than one food business.

A solicitor advising a client on the setting up of a new food business should ensure that the client is advised to register the business in time for it to trade on the anticipated day of opening because the duty is to register within 28 days before the trading day. This is so that the premises can be inspected before the business opens its doors to the public. Also, where there is a change of proprietor, the local authority must be notified before, on or within 28 days after the date of the change. This obligation rests with the new proprietor. Changes in the nature of the business must be notified by the proprietor of the business no later than 28 days after they occur. Failure to comply with these obligations is an offence under the regulations.

The regulations set out the information required for registration which includes the name, address and telephone number of the premises, the type of business, and the types of food handled. Further information is required about any vehicles, stalls and ships. The application form also requires information about the proprietors and managers of the business, whether or not it is seasonal and the number of persons employed.

Local authorities must make application forms available. Registration is free and there is no provision under the regulations enabling local authorities to refuse or review registration or to issue registration certificates. The owner of a food business must notify the local authority of any changes to the registration information, and it is an offence not to do so. Local authorities must maintain a register, which may be computerised, and which is open to public inspection at reasonable times free of charge. The register must contain only the name and address of the premises, the trading name and particulars of the nature of the business. Other information remains confidential but is to be made available for inspection by other food authorities, the police and Customs and Excise.

All food businesses are required to register, although provision is made for registration by the person who permits the use of premises used by several businesses. Provision is further made for registration of food vehicles and stalls, either at the place from which they operate or where they are stored.

Exemptions from registration

Certain premises, vehicles and stalls are exempt from the registration requirements (reg 3). These include food premises already licensed or registered under other legislation, such as slaughterhouses and dairies. Where premises are used irregularly, ie less than five days in any five consecutive weeks, there is no requirement to register. It should be noted, however, that the five days do not have to be consecutive. Thus, premises used regularly once per week must be registered, whereas activities, such as village fetes, some one-off markets and sporting events, do not require registration.

Similarly, premises where only low-risk activities take place, unless retail sale also takes place, are exempt. Registration is not required where game is killed for sport, eg grouse moors, fish is taken for food (but not processed), where normal farming activities take place, unless accompanied by cleaning and packing for retail sale, where honey is harvested, or where eggs are produced and packed. Livestock farms, livestock markets and shellfish harvesting areas do not require registration. Places where no food is kept, eg kitchens used only for washing up, administrative headquarters of a food business, some food businesses run from domestic premises, and some vehicles and stalls do not require registration. In other special circumstances, such as food sold through vending machines, where the main activity is not related to food, or in the case of food or drink only used for religious ceremonies, registration is also not required.

Detailed procedures are contained in *Code of Practice No 11: Enforcement of the Food Premises (Registration) Regulations*, which covers the administrative issues involved, including action on receipt of registration forms, provisions of the Data Protection Act 1984, retention of registration forms, supplementary records, keeping the register and supplementary records up to date, access to the register, registration certificates, charging, transmission of information to other authorities (England and Wales), deciding whether to prosecute and the uses of the register.

Supplementary records

The regulations require registration authorities to keep, as a supplementary record, the information supplied by the proprietor of a food business on the registration form which is not available to the public. If a computer system is used for the register, the registration authority should ensure that the supplementary record is not publicly accessible.

The guidance indicates that registration authorities may also wish to keep information in the supplementary record which they collect during inspections or other food law enforcement work.

This might include some or all of the following:

(a) type of food handled;
(b) number of staff trained in basic food hygiene;
(c) details of previous inspections;
(d) action taken following an inspection, for example, issue of improvement or prohibition notices;
(e) details of any complaints received;
(f) details of offences committed and convictions under the legislation;
(g) language of preference of the proprietor if it is not English (both orally and written); and
(h) the assessment of the potential risk represented by the premises.

Chapter 7

Powers of Authorised Officers

Introduction

Authorised officers have wide ranging powers under the FSA. These powers must be used correctly in accordance with both the Act and any relevant statutory code of practice to which the authorised officer must have regard under s 40(2). Food authorities have lost cases at the prosecution stage because of failure to follow the procedures laid down under the Act and in the statutory codes. Defence lawyers may seek to take advantage of instances in which food authority officers may have exceeded their statutory powers.

Powers of entry

General and specific powers of entry

The provisions relating to powers of entry by authorised officers have always existed in protective legislation, such as the FSA and the various Public Health Acts. However s 32 of the FSA incorporates a number of new powers relating to the type of premises which can be entered inside or outside the area of the authorised officer's employing authority, and the power to inspect records without necessarily requiring them as evidence, including those kept on a computer. Guidance on the powers of entry of authorised officers under s 32 is provided by *Code of Practice No 2: Legal Matters.*

Authorised officers of an enforcement authority have a right of entry, at all reasonable hours and, if so required, on production of some duly authenticated document, in three circumstances.

First, under s 32(1)(a), authorised officers are entitled to enter any premises in order to ascertain whether there is or has been any

107

contravention of the Act or regulations or order made under it. This right to enter any premises is exercisable only within the authority's area. 'Premises' is defined in s 1(3) of the Act as including 'any place, any vehicle, stall or movable structure'. The provisions of s 32(1)(a) enable authorised offices to gain access to premises in order to exercise their duty to enforce food safety law through routine inspection of premises. Indeed, there is a duty under reg 8 of the Food Safety (General Food Hygiene) Regulations 1995 and reg 19 of the Food Safety (Temperature Control) Regulations 1995 for each food authority to ensure that food premises are inspected with a frequency commensurate with their associated risk. Reference should also be made to *Code of Practice No 3* dealing with inspection procedures generally, including the general principle from the Official Control of Foodstuffs Directive that inspections should be carried out without prior notice.

Secondly, a right of entry for the purposes of investigation is given under s 32(1)(b) which provides that authorised officers have a right of entry to collect evidence for use in possible court proceedings of any contravention of the Act or regulations or orders made under it. This right is restricted to entering business premises but those premises can be situated either inside or outside the authority's area. 'Business premises' is not specifically defined in the Act, although there are statutory definitions of 'business' and 'premises' (s 1(3) of the Act). Courts are likely to give the phrase its ordinary and natural meaning in the light of those definitions.

Authorised officers should ensure that evidence collected in pursuance of this right of entry is obtained in a manner which makes it admissible in court. However, the court will decide whether such evidence is admissible after assessing whether its probative value outweighs its prejudicial effect on the defendant.

Finally, an authorised officer of a food authority is entitled to enter any premises wherever they are situated, in order to perform the authority's functions under the FSA (s 32(1)(c)).

'Authorised officer' is defined in s 5(6) as meaning any person (whether or not an officer of a food authority) who is authorised by that authority in writing either generally or specifically, to act on matters arising under the Act. A 'food authority' is one prescribed by s 5(1) of the FSA and an 'enforcement authority' is defined in s 6(1) as the authority which enforces the provisions of the Act or any regulation or order made under it. In practice, the enforcement authority is the food authority which has a duty to enforce within its area any duties not specifically imposed on some other authority (s 6(2)).

Proof of identity

An authorised officer is not obliged to show some form of identity unless requested (s 32(1)). However, this should be standard practice from both the viewpoint of the officer and the business. Businesses should instruct their staff in writing to ask to see the identity document of anyone purporting to act on behalf of the authorities. Many authorities employ technical officers/assistants who do not have the same status as an authorised officer under the FSA. It is important for the defence to know whether this can be a ground of challenge in the event of a prosecution.

The identity document must be 'some duly authenticated document', ie one of the documents covered by the provisions of s 49 of the FSA since it has to be 'given' by the food authority. Accordingly, it must be in written form and must be signed on behalf of the authority by a 'proper officer' (the officer appointed for the particular purpose by the authority) or by any officer authorised in writing by the authority to sign documents of a particular kind or a particular document. Any document signed by such a person is deemed, unless the contrary is proved, to be given under the authority of the food authority (s 49(4)).

LACOTS have produced guidance for enforcement officers on the content and format of authorisation documents. It recommends that there are six important details which it should include: the name of the authority and the appropriate department; the title of the statute, ie Food Safety Act 1990; the full name of the officer, his signature, job title and photograph; a statement that the officer is 'authorised' and has 'authority to enter premises'; the name, signature and title of the 'proper officer' authorising the enforcement officer; and the date the officer was authorised. Additional information may also be included such as the specific sections of the Act under which the officer is authorised; that he has power to enter at all reasonable times; a telephone number if there are any questions regarding the identification of the officer and his credentials; that obstructing an officer is an offence, and giving the maximum penalties.

What is reasonable

The powers of entry are only exercisable during 'reasonable hours' (s 32(1)). What is reasonable is a question of fact (see *Small v Bickley* (1875) 32 LT 726; *Davies v Winstanley* (1930) 144 LT 433).

Private dwellings

Private dwelling houses may be used for the purposes of a food business. Admission to any premises used only as a private dwelling house is not permitted as of right — rather than with a warrant — unless 24 hours' notice of the intended entry has been given to the occupier (s 32(1)).

Where an attempt is made to enter without the requisite notice having been given, the authorised officer could be refused entry and this would not constitute obstruction under s 33. Although there is no prescribed form for giving notice of intended entry, such notice should be given by letter, accompanied by proof of delivery, eg by hand or recorded delivery. The occupier need not necessarily be the owner of the house.

Entry with a warrant

The rights of entry given by s 32(1) can only be exercised with the co-operation of the occupier of the relevant premises. Section 32(2) provides the mechanism by which authorised officers can gain entry to premises where co-operation is not forthcoming. Under s 32(2), the authorised officer may in a sworn written information request a justice of the peace to issue a warrant authorising the authorised officer to enter the premises for any of the purposes in s 32(1), using reasonable force if necessary. The justice of the peace must be satisfied that there is reasonable ground for entering the premises for any of these purposes and either (a) that admission to the premises has been refused, or the authorised officer apprehends that admission will be refused and that notice of intention to apply for a warrant has been given to the occupier; or (b) that applying for admission, or giving notice of application for a warrant, would defeat the object of entry or the case is urgent or the premises are unoccupied or the occupier is temporarily absent. Warrants issued pursuant to s 32(2) continue in force for one month (s 32(3)).

Entry by other persons

An authorised officer entering any premises pursuant to s 32(1), or with a warrant issued under s 32(2), may take with him any persons he considers necessary (eg technical officers, experts, the police) (s 32(4)). The authorised officer who enters unoccupied premises with a warrant, must leave them as effectively secured against unauthorised entry as he found them (s 32(4)).

Inspection of records

An authorised officer entering premises under s 32(1) or with a warrant issued under s 32(1), may inspect any record (in any form) relating to a food business and if the records are computerised:

(a) may have access to, and inspect and check the operation of, any computer and any associated apparatus or material which is or has been in use in connection with the records; and

(b) may require any person having charge of, or otherwise concerned with the operation of, the computer, apparatus or material to give him reasonable help in discharging his duties (s 32(5)) – ie assistance must be requested from a competent person.

What is reasonable is a question of fact. For example, it would not be reasonable if a request for assistance had the effect of disrupting the proper operation of the business, for instance, requiring shutdown of a computerised till system during business hours.

Seizure and detention of records

Any officer exercising any power conferred by s 32(5) above (ie inspection of records) may seize and detain any records which he has reason to believe may be required as evidence in relevant proceedings and, where the records are computerised, may require the records to be produced in a form in which they may be taken away (s 32(6)).

It is clear that it is the authorised officer who must have grounds for believing that he needs such records as evidence. Accordingly, it would be inappropriate for a technical officer to inspect the record and form that belief on his own. The requirement for records to be produced in a form in which they may be taken away would include, for instance, downloading on to a disk.

In *Dudley Metropolitan Borough Council v Debenhams plc* (1994) *The Times*, 16 August, the Divisional Court held that a routine inspection under s 29 of the Consumer Protection Act 1987 was a 'search' within the ordinary meaning of the word and the provisions of Code B of the Police and Criminal Evidence Act 1984 (s 66) Codes of Practice relating to search of premises and seizure of property applied. The facts were that enforcement officers entered Debenhams store to ascertain whether there had been any contraventions of the Consumer Protection Act 1987 under powers conferred by s 29(1) and (2) of that Act to enter the premises. They did not have the power to require an employee to provide a business record and so, when they requested a computer printout, they were dependent on its being given to them voluntarily. The Court held that, in this situation, an employee should, pursuant to Code B, be given a notice of the powers and rights of search and should be told that he/she was not obliged to consent to the request.

Code B applies to searches of premises in three circumstances: with the occupier's consent when investigating an alleged offence; the use by the police of their powers of arrest and search under a search warrant. The implications of this judgment for the exercise of statutory powers has been vigorously criticised by LACOTS (see Circular FS 7 95). As a result of lobbying, Code B was amended to state:

> 'The Code does not apply to the exercise of a statutory power to enter premises or to inspect goods, equipment or procedures if the exercise of that power is not dependent on the existence of grounds for suspecting that an offence may have been committed and the person exercising the power has no reasonable grounds for suspicion.'

Although LACOTS welcomed this amendment, they were critical that it did not address the application of Code B to circumstances where statutory powers are exercised after suspicion that an offence has been committed or where the power itself is not sufficiently wide to cover the enquiries which officers wish to make. LACOTS' view is that Code B only applies in the limited circumstances where officers are not acting under a statutory power in which case consent to the search would be required. Some enforcement authorities consider that Code B is applicable to all routine inspections after receipt of a complaint and they have instituted the use of standard notices informing occupiers of their rights. To achieve uniformity of enforcement practice, LACOTS has drafted and circulated to all enforcement authorities two standard forms of notice, one relating to searches under statutory powers after receipt of a complaint and the other to searches carried out without statutory powers where consent is required. Whether or not an authority uses notices, as a matter of good practice, LACOTS recommends that all enforcement officers should explain the nature of any visit, the rights of occupiers and any means of appeal on enforcement decisions.

The provisions of s 32 of the FSA confer on enforcement officers wide powers of enforcement. Section 32(5) specifically confers on such officers power to inspect any 'records' including those held on a computer, a power which was not available under the Consumer Protection Act 1987 to the officers in the *Dudley* case. Nevertheless, there may be situations where those powers are not sufficiently wide to cover the particular circumstances in which case it would be prudent for the enforcement officer to use a notice. Defence solicitors should consider in all cases whether the enforcement officer had the necessary statutory powers to carry out his inspection and any seizure or detention of goods or records, to test whether a challenge such as was made in the *Dudley* case is possible.

Confidentiality of information

The disclosure of a trade secret by any person who enters the premises under s 32 is an offence under s 32(7). It is a defence if the disclosure was made in performance of a duty. A breach of confidentiality by any such person is an offence triable either way and the penalties are a maximum fine in the Magistrates Court of £5,000 or six months' imprisonment or both (s 35(2)). In a Crown Court, an offender may be sentenced to an unlimited fine or two years' imprisonment or both.

An officer of a food authority is not personally liable for any act done in the execution or purported execution of the FSA and within the scope of his employment if the act was done in the honest belief that his duty under the Act required or entitled him to do it (s 44(1)).

Obstruction of officers

The most common form of obstruction is refusal of entry. In such cases, an authorised officer may make an application for a warrant to enter the premises (s 32(2)). Reasonable force may be used to enter premises with a warrant. Such a warrant continues in force for a period of one month. The officer may also ask for police assistance, such as a police escort.

Obstruction, particularly in the case of police officers entering premises, has attracted much case law over the years. Obstruction need not involve physical violence, but must be intentional.

There are two fundamentally distinct offences under s 33(1), namely:

(a) intentionally obstructing; and

(b) failing without reasonable excuse to give information and assistance.

So anyone who intentionally obstructs any person acting in the execution of the Act, or who, without reasonable cause, fails to give any person acting in the execution of the Act any assistance or information which that person may reasonably require of him under the Act, will be guilty of an offence (s 33(1)).

The equivalent section of the Food Act 1984 used the word 'wilfully'. An act is 'wilful' if it is done deliberately rather than accidentally or inadvertently (*R v Senior* [1899] 1 QB 283 at 290–1 *per* Lord Russell of Killowen). The prosecution must prove that the defendant intended to obstruct, so that if the defendant intervened without intending to obstruct, no offence would be committed (*Wilmott v Atack* [1977] QB 498). In *Rice v Connolly* [1966] 2 QB 414, the Divisional Court held that 'wilful' meant not only intentional but without lawful excuse. In the case of obstruction, physical violence is not required before an obstruction takes place (see *Hinchliffe v Sheldon* [1955] 3 All ER 406). Moreover, 'obstructs' in s 51(3) of the Police Act 1964 means doing anything which makes it more difficult for the police to carry out their duty (*Rice v Connolly* [1966] 2 QB 414; see also *Wilmott v Atack* [1976] 3 All ER 794; *Moore v Green* [1983] 1 All ER 663; *Hills v Ellis* [1983] 1 QB 680, *Lewis v Cox* [1984] 3 All ER 672).

In *McMillan v Lackie* [1960] SLT 2, a barman working for a private club refused to supply whisky to a local authority sampling officer on the grounds that he was not allowed to supply drinks to non-members or visitors. He was held guilty of obstruction.

The word 'information' used in s 33(1)(b) includes records. In *Barge v British Gas Corporation* [1983] LGR 53, proceedings were brought under similar provisions of the Trade Descriptions Act 1968 with regard to the obstruction of authorised officers. A trading standards officer investigating a complaint asked for a copy of a document to be made for him. Office staff refused, although they did not necessarily prevent him from making and retaining a copy personally. It was alleged that there was a failure properly to comply with a request made by an authorised officer in that the office staff had failed to supply a document which the authorised officer had reason to believe might be required as evidence. The defendants were found guilty but, on appeal, it was held that an offence under s 29(1)(b) of the Trade Descriptions Act 1968 was committed only where there was a wilful failure to comply with a requirement made by the authorised officer under s 28 of that Act. The section, properly construed, did not entitle an authorised officer to require an individual to hand over documents and, since in this case the only demand made was to supply documents, the requirement had been complied with and no offence had been committed.

False or misleading information

Any person from whom information is requested who knowingly or recklessly provides false or misleading information commits an offence under s 33(2).

The above offences are punishable, summarily only, under s 35(1) of the FSA. The penalty is a maximum fine of £5,000 or imprisonment for not more than three months or both. The time limits for prosecutions under the Act set out in s 34 do not apply to offences under s 33(1). Accordingly, the time limit for prosecution of such offences is six months from the time when the offence was committed (s 127 of the Magistrates' Courts Act 1980). Failure to prosecute within the time limit may be an abuse of process (see Chapter 5, pp 72–4).

Self-incrimination and the giving of information

Nothing in s 33(1)(b) can compel anyone to answer any question or give any information if to do so might incriminate him (s 33(3)).

Under the common law a potential defendant has an unqualified right of silence known as the privilege against self-incrimination.

This means that he cannot be compelled to answer questions or provide information if to do so would expose him to liability for a criminal offence. In recent years, the common law right has been eroded by the courts holding in certain areas that the relevant legislation has impliedly abrogated the privilege against self-incrimination. However, in the field of trading law, many statutes have expressedly preserved the privilege and s 33(5) of the Act is an example of this.

Section 33(5) falls into two parts: answering questions and giving information. In relation to answering questions, where an authorised officer interviews a suspect (rather than a witness to the commission of the offence) and has grounds to suspect that the person has committed an offence, he must caution that person as follows:

> 'You do not have to say anything, but it may harm your defence if you do not mention when questioned something which you later rely on in court. Anything you do say may be given in evidence.'

The officer must comply with the provisions of the Police and Criminal Evidence Act 1984 (PACE) Code C which relates to interviewing. LACOTS *Guidance for Dealing with Food Complaints made to Local Authority Environmental Health Departments* incorporates recommendations on the implementation of PACE Code C. This caution should not be confused with what is known as a formal caution used as an alternative to prosecution (see Chapter 3).

The word 'give' in s 33(3) is significant. It implies that someone must be asked to hand over information. Accordingly, anything seized is not covered by the right against self-incrimination and a food proprietor cannot seek to prevent the seizure of records on his premises on the grounds that such records may contain material which may incriminate him (see *Rank Film Distributors v Video Information Centre* [1982] AC 380, where the House of Lords upheld the seizure of documents under an Anton Piller order). However, if it is information which is *requested* by the authorised officer, the food proprietor can rely on the sub-section. The officer will then have to obtain the evidence by other means.

Although para 14 of the *Code of Practice No 2: Legal Matters* reminds officers that s 33(3) 'provides that no person shall be required to incriminate himself', defendants should only rely upon s 33(3) only with good cause. Unfortunately, keeping silent often results in greater suspicion and it may be wise for the proprietor to disclose information, especially where the information's potentially detrimental effect is marginal.

Section 33(1)(b) refers to 'assistance or information' and it is submitted that the word 'information' in s 33(3) includes any documentation because of the contrast between it and asking questions.

The case of *Snape v Mulvenna* ((1994) *The Times*, 28 December) highlights that the privilege against self-incrimination is only available to the person who may have committed the relevant offence, not to a witness. In *Snape v Mulvenna*, the Divisional Court considered the question of obstruction and its interrelationship with the privilege against self-incrimination in the context of s 32 of the Consumer Protection Act 1987. A trading standards officer was investigating a misleading price indication for bananas where he was charged 19p per pound at the till as opposed to 29p as indicated in the shop. The till assistant, Miss Snape, was requested to give an interview but she refused on the instructions of her supervisors. She was charged with obstruction. Section 47 of the Consumer Protection Act 1987 contains a privilege against self-incrimination provision virtually identical to s 33(3). However, the magistrates held that Miss Snape had not relied on that section, that an employer cannot lawfully instruct an employee not to answer questions and she was convicted, although given an absolute discharge. The Divisional Court upheld the conviction, also holding that Miss Snape had not refused to answer questions in reliance on the privilege against self-incrimination because the misleading price offence was one alleged against her employer, not against her and, therefore, the privilege was not available to her. As Butler-Sloss LJ remarked, Miss Snape 'was caught between the devil and the deep blue sea'. She risked committing the offence of obstruction or disobeying the instructions of her superiors. Sadly, someone in Miss Snape's position cannot rely on s 33(3) for it is clear that this section only applies to the person who is alleged to have committed the offence and not to persons who are merely witnesses and from whom enforcement officers seek information.

Chapter 8

Methods of Enforcement

This chapter deals with the statutory enforcement methods available to the food authorities, the courts and the ministers. These include the powers of authorised officers to serve and enforce improvement notices and emergency prohibition notices, together with existing powers of inspection and seizure of suspected food. Courts can make prohibition orders and emergency prohibition orders and the minister can make emergency control orders.

As seen from previous chapters, every food authority is charged with the duty to enforce the FSA within its area. Section 6(2) and regulations provide similar duties.

The main methods of enforcement by food authorities are dealt with in s 9 (inspection and seizure of food), s 10 (improvement notices), s 11 (prohibition orders), s 12 (emergency prohibition notices and orders) and s 13 (emergency control orders).

The statutory provisions are supplemented by Codes of Practice made under s 40 of the FSA, the purpose of which are to endeavour to achieve consistency of enforcement by the different enforcement authorities. The legal status of these codes is discussed in Chapter 1.

In enforcing the Food Safety (General Food Hygiene) Regulations 1995 and the Food Safety (Temperature Control) Regulations 1995 each food authority is required to take into account whether there has been compliance with any relevant guide to good hygiene practice developed in compliance with art 5 of Council Directive 93/43/EEC of 14 June 1993 on the hygiene of foodstuffs (see reg 8 of the FSGFHR and reg 19 of the FSTCR).

Inspection, seizure and detention of food

Section 9 contains the legal procedures for the inspection and subsequent seizure by an authorised officer of suspect food. It extends existing provisions relating to the powers of inspectors to inspect food at all reasonable times, at any stage between manufacture and distribution, to ascertain its compliance with food safety requirements as specified in s 8(2).

Procedures covering the inspection, detention and seizure of food are covered by statutory *Code of Practice No 4: Inspection, Detention and Seizure of Suspect Food*. This code provides advice and guidance on when to use detention and seizure powers and the procedures for dealing with different batches and types of food, including security arrangements, particularly where there is a risk that the food may be tampered with. In such cases, it may be necessary for the food to be locked in a room or enclosure, sealed or marked in such a way that removal of part is obvious and/or requires the presence of security personnel. Generally the food should not be left in the charge of, or in premises owned by, any person who may be prosecuted for an offence under s 7 or 8 of the FSA.

Inspection of food

Section 9(1) empowers an authorised officer of a food authority at all reasonable times to inspect any food intended for human consumption which:

(a) has been sold or is offered or exposed for sale;
(b) is in the possession of, or has been deposited with or consigned to, any person for the purpose of sale or preparation for sale.

For discussion of the terms 'sale', 'exposure' and 'intended for human consumption', see Chapter 2. 'At all reasonable times' is a question of fact.

The term 'inspect' is not defined in the FSA, but is related to the requirements of the Council Directive 89/337/EEC on the official control of foodstuffs in relation to inspection procedures. *Code of Practice No 3: Inspection Procedures – General* advises food authorities on procedures for undertaking inspections, including programmed inspection, notice of inspection, co-ordination of inspection visits, operating in other local authority areas and post-inspection procedures. Under this code of practice and, when not otherwise stated, for the purpose of other codes issued under the Act, 'inspection' means visiting and inspecting premises and inspecting equipment (including cleaning and maintenance equipment); inspecting a process or operational procedures; inspecting the hygiene or practices of personnel; inspecting food (including ingredients, additives and products at any stage of manufacture) or contact materials, and inspecting labels, labelling requirements and advertising material and/or records.

Taking appropriate samples and their subsequent analysis and/or examination often forms an integral part of inspection, particularly the inspection of factories.

Generally, authorised officers visit premises in two circumstances. First, they may visit in response to a particular complaint, to take samples and to check compliance with an enforcement notice, such as an Improvement Notice. *Code of Practice No 2: Legal Matters* outlines the procedures to be followed. Secondly, an authorised officer may visit premises to undertake one or both of two types of inspection – a food standards inspection and/or a food hygiene inspection. Procedures to be followed by authorised officers are detailed in *Code of Practice No 8: Food Standards Inspections* and *Code of Practice No 9: Food Hygiene Inspections* (revised September 1995). Once the authorised officer has carried out the inspection, he has a choice in dealing with any unfit food. He can either withdraw or detain the food in question or seize it.

Acting without inspection

Similar powers are given where it appears that food may cause food poisoning or a disease communicable to human beings in circumstances not arising from actual inspection of the food (s 9(2)). *Code of Practice No 4: Inspection, Detention and Seizure of Suspect Food* advises authorised officers that s 9(2) may apply equally to food which has not been inspected. This would occur when it appears to the officer that the food is so contaminated that it is likely to cause food poisoning or any disease communicable to human beings. In such cases, the authorised officer may act to seize or detain the food without an inspection if, for example, information is received from another reliable source, eg other food authorities, public health laboratory service or central government, that the food may be contaminated or cause food poisoning or any communicable disease. In these circumstances, inspection is not required by law but it may be necessary to inspect the food if only for identification purposes. In the non-metropolitan counties, this provision should only be used by authorised officers of the district councils (paras 29 and 30 of *Code of Practice No 4*).

Detention or seizure of food

Where it appears to an authorised officer after inspecting food that it fails to comply with food safety requirements (s 9(1)) or, without inspecting the food, that, is likely to cause food poisoning or any disease communicable to human beings (s 9(2)); he has a discretionary power to exercise one of two methods of enforcement, namely detention of the food or seizure of it. Section 9(3) provides that the authorities officer may either:

(a) give notice to the person in charge of the food that, until the notice is withdrawn, the food or any specified portion of it is not to be used for human consumption and either must not be removed or, alternatively, removed to a place specified in the notice (s 9(3)(a)); or

(b) seize the food and remove it in order to have it dealt with by a justice of the peace (s 9(3)(b)).

Any person who knowingly contravenes the requirements of a detention notice under para (a) above is guilty of an offence. For an offence to be committed, the prosecution must prove that the person to whom notice was given intended to contravene the requirements of the notice (see the use of the word 'knowingly', see s 9(3)).

Paragraph 20 of *Code of Practice No 4: Inspection, Detention and Seizure of Suspect Food* advises enforcement authorities that only appropriately qualified authorised officers should take the decision to detain or seize food.

Detention of food

The authorised officer must give notice to the person in charge of the food (s 9(3)(a)). To do this, the officer must serve a Notice of Detention form (reproduced in Appendix 2) prescribed by the Detention of Food (Prescribed Forms) Regulations 1990 (SI 1990 No 2614) (see s 49(1) and (2)). Failure to use the prescribed form is a material irregularity. The Notice of Detention must be signed by or on behalf of the authorised officer who took the decision to detain the food (para 21 of *Code of Practice No 4: Inspection, Detention and Seizure of Suspect Food*). This is because, reading ss 9(1), 9(2) and 9(3), the duty to give notice is imposed on the authorised officer to whom it appeared that the food did not comply with food safety requirements or was likely to cause food poisoning or a communicable disease.

Where an authorised officer exercises the powers conferred by subs (3)(a) above, he must, as soon as is reasonably practicable and in any event within 21 days, determine whether or not he is satisfied that the food complies with the food safety requirements and, if he is so satisfied must immediately withdraw the notice (s 9(4)(a)). He must do so by using a Withdrawal of Detention of Food Notice form (reproduced in Appendix 2) as prescribed by the Detention of Food (Prescribed Forms) Regulations 1990. It is the authorised officer who exercised the original power to detain the food who must satisfy himself whether or not the food safety requirements are complied with. The Withdrawal of Detention of Food Notice must be signed by or on behalf of that authorised officer. The notice withdrawing the detention must be served as soon as possible to prevent further deterioration of the food. The notice need not be served by the officer who made the decision to detain the food. It may be served by any competent person (see paras 22 and 28 of *Code of Practice No 4: Inspection, Detention and Seizure of Suspect Food*). Where he is not satisfied, he must seize the food and serve a Food Condemnation Warning Notice (reproduced in Appendix 2) as prescribed by the Detention of Food (Prescribed Forms) Regulations 1990 and take the food before a magistrate.

Seizure of food

Authorised officers may seize food in two circumstances. First, s 9(3) provides a discretionary power to an authorised officer who has inspected food and formed the opinion that it fails to comply with food safety requirements (s 9(1)) or, having not inspected the food, it appears to him that it is likely to cause food poisoning or a disease communicable to human beings (s 9(2)), to seize the food and remove it in order to have it dealt with by a magistrate. Secondly, where the authorised officer originally detained the food and then decides in accordance with the provisions of s 9(4) that he is not satisfied that the food complies with food safety requirements, he has no choice but to seize the food and to remove it to be dealt with by a magistrate (s 9(4)(b)).

Where the authorised officer intends to use his power to seize food, he must inform the person in charge of the food of his intention to have it dealt with by a magistrate: s 9(5). Section 9(5) does not require a notice to be served but paragraph 20 of *Code of Practice No 4: Inspection, Detention and Seizure of Suspect Food* advises officers to confirm seizure in writing immediately. A Food Condemnation Warning Notice should be used as prescribed by the Detention of Food (Prescribed Forms) Regulations 1990.

Authorised officers should have regard to the chain of evidence where this might be crucial in any subsequent prosecutions and should do everything possible not to leave the food which has been seized unattended (para 23 of *Code of Practice No 4: Inspection, Detention and Seizure of Suspect Food*).

Service of notices

Service of notices under s 9 must comply with the provisions of s 50 of the FSA. Notices may be served as follows:

(a) by delivering it to the relevant person; or

(b) in the case of an incorporated company or body, by delivering it to their secretary or clerk at their registered or principal office, or by sending it in a prepaid letter addressed to that person at that office; or

(c) in the case of any other person, by leaving it, or sending it in a prepaid letter addressed to that person, at his usual or last known residence.

However, para 25 of *Code of Practice No 4: Inspection, Detention and Seizure of Suspect Food* recommends that notices used in the enforcement of s 9 should be served by hand on the person in charge of the food, and its owner should be notified if practicable. Time should be allowed for witnesses to be contacted before having the food dealt with by a magistrate. Up to two days may be allowed in this case unless the food is highly perishable, in which event it should be dealt with as soon as possible (para 26 of *Code of Practice No 4*). The person in charge of the food or the owner should be allowed to be present when the food is dealt with by a magistrate.

Informing the person in charge

Where an authorised officer exercises the seizure powers conferred by s 9(3)(b) or (4)(b) above, he must inform the person in charge of the food of his intention to have it dealt with by a magistrate. Any person who under s 7 or 8 of the FSA might be liable to prosecution in respect of the food will, if he attends before the magistrate dealing with the case, be entitled to be heard and call witnesses (s 9(5)(a)). Paragraph 11 of *Code of Practice No 4* recommends that, after a Food Condemnation Warning Notice is served, the magistrate should deal with the food in question within two days or as soon as possible if the food is of a highly perishable nature. The practicalities of obtaining the services of a magistrate must also be considered. It is essential that authorised officers establish a formal liaison with the local court to ensure that a magistrate can be made available at short notice (see paras 45 to 50 of *Code of Practice No 4*).

The role of the magistrate

The role of the magistrate is particularly important when witnesses are being heard. In *Humphrey v Errington* (unreported) which involved Lanark Blue cheese, the Court of Session in Scotland held that in exercising powers under s 9, the magistrate was acting in a judicial and not in an administrative capacity (see *R v Cornwall Quarter Sessions ex p Kerley* [1956] 1 WLR 906 where it was held that a magistrate acted as 'superior inspector' who reviewed the decision of the authorised officer that the food should be condemned and therefore acted in an administrative capacity). See also *R v Birmingham City Justices ex p Chris Foreign Foods (Wholesalers) Ltd* [1970] 3 All ER 945 which established that, even though the magistrate does not act as a judge, he must act fairly when making his decision). The magistrate may, but need not, be a member of the court before which any person is charged with an offence under ss 7 and 8 in relation to that food (s 9(5)(b)). This provision does not apply in Scotland (s 9(9)(b)).

The magistrate must hear the evidence from both sides and decide whether to condemn the food and order its destruction or disposal to prevent it being used for human consumption. The fact that the magistrate does condemn the food is not conclusive proof that it was unfit for human consumption (*Waye v Thompson* (1885) 15 QBD 342). There is no statutory right of appeal against the decision of a magistrate to condemn food. However, such a decision can be challenged by way of judicial review. Grounds for such a review include:

    (a) a failure by the magistrate to take relevant matters into account;

    (b) the magistrate taking irrelevant matters into account;

(c) the magistrate reaching a decision which is so irrational that no magistrate could reach it;

(d) the adoption of an unfair procedure which fails to adhere to the principles of natural justice; or

(e) the magistrate was biased.

In *Humphrey v Errington*, the sheriff's failure to allow the defendant to call expert witness was a denial of natural justice.

Where the magistrate condemns the food, he may also order that expenses incurred by the food authority in connection with disposal or destruction be defrayed by the owner of the food (s 9(6)(b)). Conversely, if the notice is withdrawn by the food authority or the magistrate refuses to condemn the food in question, the food authority must compensate the owner for any depreciation in its value resulting from the action taken by the authorised officer (s 9(7)). Any dispute about the right to or the amount of any compensation payable under subs (7) must be referred to arbitration (s 9(8)).

Section 9(9) sets out how the application of s 9 differs in Scotland. In Scotland, any reference in s 9 to a magistrate includes a reference to the sheriff and to a magistrate. Paragraph (b) of subs (5) does not apply, any order made under subs (6) is sufficient evidence in any proceedings under the Act of the failure of the food in question to comply with food safety requirements, and the reference in subs (8) to determination by arbitration means a reference to determination by a single arbiter appointed by the sheriff if the parties cannot agree.

Disposal or destruction of food

Food authorities are responsible for organising the destruction or disposal of food. This may be by total destruction, eg incineration, or disfigurement of the food commodity, eg flattening cans prior to disposal in a landfill site. Security provisions should ensure that such food cannot be returned to the food supply chain.

Batches, lots or consignments of food

Under s 8(3), where any food which fails to comply with the food safety requirements is part of a batch, lot or consignment of food of the same class or description, it shall be presumed for the purposes of s 9, until the contrary is proved, that all of the food in the batch, lot or consignment fails to comply with those requirements. Paragraph 32 of *Code of Practice No 4* advises authorised officers that they need reliable evidence before taking action but, if there are serious doubts about the safety of the food, the whole batch, lot or consignment should be detained. Part of the food may be seized later and then the notice may be withdrawn in respect of the remainder, if the officer is satisfied or has evidence from, for example, the public analyst or food examiner, that the problem affects *only part* of the batch, lot or consignment.

Paragraph 33 of *Code of Practice No 4* states that, when considering whether to seize or detain food which is part of a batch, lot or consignment, authorised officers must take the following into account:

(a) the nature of the contamination;
(b) the nature and condition of any container holding the food;
(c) the risk to health;
(d) the evidence available; and
(e) the quantity of food involved in relation to any sampling which has been undertaken.

Reference in regard to suspect batches and lots should be made to the Food (Lot Marking) Regulations 1992 (SI 1992 No 1357) made to implement Council Directive 89/396/EEC on batch identification; s 13 of the FSA (emergency control orders) (see below); and *Code of Practice No 16* on the operation of the Food Hazard Warning System.

Voluntary surrender procedures

The practice of voluntary surrender of food by an owner to the food authority has been in operation for many years. This may be on the instigation of the owner or the authorised officer. Where food is voluntarily surrendered for destruction, a receipt should be issued and the description of the food should include the phrase 'voluntarily surrendered for destruction'. The receipt should be signed by the person surrendering the food.

Improvement notices

Under previous food legislation, there was no provision for the service of notices by authorised officers to deal with situations which did not necessarily warrant prosecution. Now there is power under s 10 of the FSA to serve improvement notices to remedy breaches of regulations.

Advice to enforcement officers on procedures relating to improvement notices is contained in statutory *Code of Practice No 5: The Use of Improvement Notices* (revised April 1994). The issue of an improvement notice does not preclude the food authority from pursuing prosecution at the same time for the breaches of the regulations which are the subject of the notice. The improvement notice procedure is designed to ensure that the defects are remedied as quickly as possible.

An improvement notice should only be served when the authorised officer is satisfied that there has been a contravention of one of the relevant food hygiene or food processing regulations but that the contravention does not pose an imminent risk to health. It is important that those regulations to which ss 10 and 11 of the FSA apply are identified. They were originally identified in the Schedule to *Code of Practice No 6* but the list needs to be updated. The document issued in October 1995 by the Ministry of Agriculture, Fisheries and Food (MAFF) entitled *Food Law* identifies all the current regulations and is available through the MAFF Food Safety Directorate Consumer Helpline (0345 573012)

Informal procedures

Before invoking the formal procedure under s 10, informal measures are available to enforcement officers if appropriate. The informal procedure of giving advice orally, sending advisory letters and informal warnings is well established and is accepted and understood by the food trade. For example, many food authorities use an informal type of notice which confirms details of contraventions of regulations identified particularly during the inspection of a food premises. Authorised officers may use these informal procedures provided they believe that such procedures will be as effective as those allowed for under the statutory system. Where this is the case it may be possible to negotiate the withdrawal of notices on the basis that informal procedures will achieve the improvements the authorised officer requires. In some cases, a proprietor may be advised of the outcome of an inspection by letter. It is important that letters sent by authorised officers distinguish between formal legal requirements and what is considered good hygiene practice.

Where there is a breach of a recommendation of some industry guideline or an industry code of practice, an improvement notice cannot be issued unless there is also a failure to comply with an appropriate regulation.

The notice procedure should be properly used by all authorised officers. The procedure, and particularly the appeal rights, should be properly understood by recipients. The notice may need to be accompanied by a covering letter written in the recipient's own language suggesting that he seek help if he does not fully understand the meaning of the notice, or the notice may need to be explained with the assistance of an interpreter. The issue of a notice should be treated seriously. The person receiving it should understand that he is obliged to comply with the notice and that failure to do so is an offence for which he could be prosecuted by the authority (see para 14 of *Code of Practice No 5*).

Formal procedures

Section 10 states that, if an authorised officer of an enforcement authority has reasonable grounds for believing that the proprietor of a food business is failing to comply with any regulations to which the section applies, he may serve an improvement notice on the proprietor.

Section 10(1)(d) makes it clear that works of equivalent effect may be carried out to comply with the improvement notice. It is the responsibility of the food authority to tell the proprietor this. Authorised officers should request the proprietor to discuss alternative works before they are carried out. Where alternative works are agreed, the authorised officer should confirm to the proprietor, in writing, that they have been approved (para 44 of *Code of Practice No 5*).

Under s 10(2), any person who fails to comply with an improvement notice is guilty of an offence. The offence is triable either way. Crown courts have power to imprison offenders for not more than two years and/or to impose an unlimited fine. Magistrates may only fine offenders a maximum of £5,000 and can imprison for not more than six months (s 35(2)).

Examples of improvement notices

Guidance is given in *Code of Practice No 5* as to typical situations where the service of improvement notices would be appropriate, namely:
  (a) where rodent proofing or flying insect screening is needed to prevent any risk of infestation;

(b) where the structure or facilities in the food business are deficient, eg where structural repairs are required or where additional equipment is necessary to comply with temperature control requirements;

(c) where there has been a previous history of obstruction or unwillingness to conform to legal requirements;

(d) where the facilities to wash and prepare food and to wash equipment and utensils are inadequate;

(e) where there is inadequate mechanical ventilation in a kitchen area;

(f) where there is inadequate artificial lighting in a food room; and

(g) where there is a failure to maintain premises in a satisfactory state of cleanliness.

The service of an improvement notice would not be appropriate where the contravention might be a continuing one, for example, personal cleanliness of staff, and a notice would only secure temporary improvement, or in transient situations where it is considered that swift enforcement action is needed, for example a one-day festival or sporting events, and an emergency prohibition notice or prosecution would be the only formal remedy which would have immediate effect.

Form of Notice

An improvement notice must be in the form prescribed in the Food Safety (Improvement and Prohibition – Prescribed Forms) Regulations 1991 (SI 1991 No 100) (reproduced in Appendix 2) and must, in accordance with s 10(1):

(a) state the officer's grounds for believing that the proprietor is failing to comply with the regulations;

(b) specify the matters which constitute the proprietor's failure to comply;

(c) specify the measures which, in the officer's opinion, the proprietor must take in order to secure compliance; and

(d) require the proprietor to take those measures, or measures which are at least equivalent to them, within the period (not being less than 14 days) as may be specified in the notice.

It will be seen that s 10(1) specifies four matters to be set out in the improvement notice; these are four separate matters and each must be specified. The failure to specify one matter cannot be cured by specification of another. In *Mayor and Burgesses of the London*

Borough of Bexley v Gardner Merchant Ltd [1993] COD 383, the respondent company had appealed to the magistrates against two improvement notices which failed to specify all four matters. The Divisional Court, allowing the appeal on the ground that the failure to particularise all four elements invalidated the notices, also held that if a notice does not comply with s 10(1) then the appropriate action on appeal is to cancel the improvement notice under s 39 of the FSA. It is inappropriate for the court to modify or cancel it. The reason for this is that non-compliance with an improvement notice is a criminal offence and clear and precise drafting is required in accordance with *Code of Practice No 5*.

An improvement notice specifies both the measures to be taken and the period of time within which the proprietor must implement those measures. The minimum period which may be specified is 14 days, but specified periods of time for completion of works must be realistic. In most cases, the period of time would be agreed with the proprietor although an authorised officer can set a limit without the proprietor's agreement. The following factors should be taken into account before a time limit is set:

(a) the nature of the problem;
(b) the risk to health; and
(c) the availability of solutions.

Who should issue an improvement notice?

Code of Practice No 5 recommends that improvement notices should be issued and signed only by authorised, fully qualified officers with experience in food law enforcement. These will be environmental health officers enforcing food hygiene or food processing regulations and official veterinary surgeons, designated under the Authorised Officers (Meat Inspection) Regulations 1987 (SI 1987 No 133) and carrying out official veterinary surgeon duties. Authorities need to be satisfied that officers are competent on the basis of qualifications and experience of a variety of food law enforcement situations.

Service of the notice

Section 10 requires that the improvement notice is served on the proprietor of the food business. Section 50(1) of the FSA provides for the methods by which documents required to be served by the Act, such as improvement notices, may be served. The notice may be delivered to the person or it may be left or sent in a prepaid letter addressed to that person, at his usual or last known residence. In the case of a company or other body, the notice may be delivered to its secretary or clerk at the registered or principal office or sent there by post. Of all these methods, para 27 of *Code of Practice No 5* recommends that the notice should normally be served by post and that proof of posting should be obtained. Alternatively, it should be served by hand.

Where it is not practicable after reasonable inquiry to ascertain the name and address of the proprietor, it can be served by addressing it to the 'owner' or 'occupier' and delivering it to someone on the premises or, if there is no such person, by affixing it to a conspicuous part of the premises (s 50(2)).

Paragraph 26 of *Code of Practice No 5* recommends that the person responsible for acting on the notice should receive a copy of the notice, especially in cases where the local manager is not the proprietor. An improvement notice need not necessarily be served by the authorised officer who signed it and issued it but it should be served by a competent person who would be able to take any required action, for example, explaining the purpose of the notice (para 27 of *Code of Practice No 5*).

Extension of time

Sometimes, a proprietor may request an extension of the time period for complying with an improvement notice. Paragraph 41 of *Code of Practice No 5* lists those matters which an authorised officer should take into account when deciding whether to extend time:

(a) the risk associated with the fault if an extension was granted;
(b) the reason for the request;
(c) the remedy involved;
(d) the past record of co-operation of the proprietor; and
(e) any temporary action which the proprietor proposes to take to remedy the defect.

An authorised officer, if he considers a request for an extension of time to be reasonable, may decide not to enforce the notice until a further period has elapsed. Requests for time extensions must be made in writing before the expiry date of the notice otherwise, technically, an offence will be committed if there has been failure to comply.

Appeals

The proprietor has a right of appeal against the decision of an authorised officer to serve an improvement notice by way of a complaint to the magistrates court (s 37). Appeal is made by way of complaint to the Magistrates Court pursuant to s 51 of the Magistrates' Courts Act 1980. Although the form of complaint is prescribed by the Magistrates' Courts (Forms) Rules 1981, Form 98, the complaint need not be made in writing. It can be made by the complainant personally or by his solicitor or counsel (r 4 of the Magistrates' Courts Rules 1981). Once the magistrate has judicially considered the complaint, a summons is issued. The hearing of the complaint is governed by the rules in ss 53 to 57 of the Magistrates' Courts Act 1980. The procedure in Scotland is to make a summary application to the sheriff.

The time limit for appeal against an improvement notice is one month from the date the notice was served, or the period specified in the improvement notice if that is shorter (s 37(5)).

The FSA sets out the powers of the magistrates on an appeal against an improvement notice in s 39(1). The court may cancel, affirm or modify the terms of the notice, for example, to delete or reduce what it deems to be an over-rigorous requirement or to extend the time in which the proprietor is required to comply with the notice. However, the magistrates must decide whether a notice is valid before they exercise their powers under s 39(1). If the notice is invalid, all they may do is cancel it. If it is valid, they must affirm it but may exercise their power of modification (*London Borough of Bexley v Gardner Merchant Limited* [1993] COD 383). Magistrates have no power to modify notices if this would have the effect of changing the requirements of the regulations under which the notice was served (*Salford City Council v Abbeyfield (Worsley) Society Ltd* [1993] COD 384). In this case, the magistrates' amendment to a notice to exclude residents of an old people's home from the requirement in reg 11 of the Food Hygiene (General) Regulations 1970 for food handlers to wear overclothing was declared invalid by the Divisional Court since reg 11 required *all* persons who handled food to wear overclothing. The magistrates were entitled to affirm the improvement notice with modifications but not so as to permit something in contravention of the regulations.

Magistrates have no power to rectify service of the notice on the wrong person (see Chapter 5). Where magistrates dismiss an appeal against an improvement notice, appeal lies to the Crown Court by a person aggrieved, which need not be the accused or the prosecuting authority but could be anyone legally affected by the decision (s 38 of the FSA). Appeal to the Crown Court proceeds by way of rehearing of the evidence. Appeal may also be made to the Divisional Court by way of case stated in respect of a question of law or jurisdiction (see Chapter 3, pp 18–19).

Section 39(2) provides that the recipient of the notice is not prejudiced by lodging an appeal because the appeal suspends the period of compliance until the appeal has been determined. An appeal is regarded as no longer pending if it is finally determined by the court, if the proprietor withdraws his appeal, or if the appeal is struck out because the proprietor did not pursue it expeditiously (s 39(3)).

It is essential that the recipient of a notice clearly understands that he has the right of appeal against the service of an improvement notice and the relevant information should be contained within notes attached to the notice. Details should include, for example, the name and address of the relevant local court. The proprietor should also be asked to notify the officer if an appeal is lodged. Authorised officers should be responsive to discussing the need for a notice after an appeal, especially where their interpretation is contrary to LACOTS advice.

Compliance

The FSA does not make any provision for the 'signing off' of an improvement notice by the food authority, but *Code of Practice No 5* does recommend such a procedure. Lawyers should advise their clients to notify the authorised officer when work is complete and to request re-inspection so that the authorised officer can confirm compliance. This is particularly appropriate in the case of continuing offences (see *R v Thames Metropolitan Stipendiary Magistrate ex p London Borough of Hackney* (1994) 158 JP 305).

Authorised officers are encouraged to liaise with proprietors while work is being undertaken, ensuring notification to the authority when work is completed. The work should be checked as soon as possible after notification, preferably by the officer who served the notice. Food authorities are also recommended to review the frequency of inspection of the premises after the works have been carried out bearing in mind the nature of the risk which led to the issuing of the notice.

Records

Authorities are recommended to maintain a record of the number of Improvement Notices issued. The record should list the number of notices issued in respect of a particular business, the number served in relation to a particular problem, and the effectiveness of those served.

Such information should be kept for each category of food business in accordance with guidance issued on the statistical returns under the EC Official Control of Foodstuffs Directive, to assist with future programming of routine inspections based upon risk assessments.

Prohibition procedures

General

Prior to the FSA, food authorities had limited powers to deal with high risk situations. For example, they did not have statutory powers to close premises which were insanitary or where the operation of the business exposed people to risk of food-borne illness or even death. The Act brought in a range of new powers to combat these high-risk situations, in particular allowing authorised officers to move swiftly to prevent such risks continuing.

Section 11 deals with the circumstances in which magistrates (or, in Scotland, the sheriff) may make prohibition orders. Section 12 covers the powers of an authorised officer to serve an emergency prohibition notice where there is imminent risk of injury to health in respect of premises, equipment or process, and for a court to make an emergency prohibition order. Procedures covering these aspects of enforcement are dealt with in statutory *Code of Practice No 6: Prohibition Procedures.*

Prohibition orders

Prohibition orders are the subject of s 11 of the FSA and *Code of Practice No 6*. Breach of a prohibition order is a criminal offence.

Power to impose the prohibition

Where the proprietor of a food business is convicted of an offence under any regulations to which s 11 applies (s 11(1)(a)), and the court which convicted him is satisfied that the health risk condition is fulfilled in connection with that business (s 11(1)(b)), the court must order the appropriate prohibition. The regulations to which s 11 applies are the same as for s 10 (see above). Furthermore, if a court makes an Emergency Prohibition Order under s 12 with respect to any food business, then s 11(1) applies as if a conviction had taken place under those regulations (s 11(9)).

The health risk condition

The health risk condition is fulfilled with respect to any food business if any of the following involves risk of injury to health:
  (a) the use for the purposes of the business of any process or treatment;
  (b) the construction of any premises used for the purposes of the business, or the use for those purposes of any equipment; and
  (c) the state or condition of any premises or equipment used for the purpose of the business (s 11(2)).

The appropriate prohibition

These extensive new powers allow a court, where it is satisfied that the health risk condition is fulfilled, to prohibit, respectively, the use of the process or treatment for the purpose of the business; the use of the premises or equipment for the purposes of the business or any other food business of the same class or description; or the use of the premises or equipment for the purposes of any food business (s 11(3)).

Imposition of the Prohibition Order on proprietors or managers

If the proprietor or manager of a food business is convicted of an offence under any regulations to which s 11 applies by virtue of s 10(3)(b) (ie hygiene rather than food processing regulations), the convicting court has a discretionary power to prohibit by order the proprietor or manager participating in the management of any food business, or a particular food business specified in the order (s 11(4)).

Prohibition of a person

The circumstances which may lead a court to consider prohibition of a person from participating in the management of any food business or a specified food business are covered briefly in the *Code of Practice No 6* (para 56). Such circumstances may include repeated serious offences, such as:

(a) failure to clean the premises;
(b) failure to maintain equipment;
(c) blatant disregard for health risks; or
(d) putting the public at risk by knowingly using unfit food.

Information to be given to a court

Where a prosecuting authority is seeking to prohibit a specific person from running or participating in a food business, information is required to assist the court in reaching a decision whether or not to make a prohibition order, so the officer should attend court to give evidence (para 57 of *Code of Practice No 6*).

Information which could be required includes:

(a) the state of the premises or equipment, both at the time of the offence and at the time the premises were revisited prior to the hearing;

(b) evidence that the proprietor or manager had been involved in the commission of the offences which tended to show weaknesses in management. In the latter case, the authorised officer could well investigate to ascertain whether the proprietor or manager had been involved in convictions at previous food premises and what these convictions were for. It is standard practice for those prosecuting to ascertain whether there have been any previous convictions or cautions and to obtain details for presentation to the court in the event of the prosecution being successful (para 60 of the *Code of Practice No 6*).

Action when a prohibition order has been made

For the prohibition of a person to be fully effective, other authorities should be notified as the individual may try to start a business in another area. The Chartered Institute of Environmental Health (CIEH) should be notified of the name and address of the person concerned, any names used by that person previously, the information the prosecution gave to the court which led it to make the order, any reasons given by the court for making the order and the address of the premises where the offences occurred (para 61 of *Code of Practice No 6*). The CIEH must be informed if a prohibition order is lifted (para 62 of *Code of Practice No 6*). Similar provisions apply in Scotland, where the Royal Environmental Health Institute should be notified. The CIEH will arrange for the notification of other authorities and will contact LACOTS so that authorities at county level are also aware of the prohibition.

Service of the order

As soon as practicable after making the order under s 11(1) or (4), the enforcement authority must serve a copy of the order on the proprietor of the business and in the case of an order under subs (1), fix a copy of the order in a conspicuous position at the appropriate business premises (s 11(5)).

Anyone who knowingly contravenes such an order is guilty of an offence (s 11(5)).

Duration of the order

After conviction of the proprietor of the food business and the court having made the appropriate prohibition order in respect of the business, a prohibition order ceases to have effect on the issue by the enforcement authority of a certificate that they are satisfied that the proprietor has taken sufficient measures to secure that the business no longer fulfils the health risk condition or, where the proprietor or manager has been prohibited from participating in the management of any food business, on the court giving a direction to that effect (s 11(6)). In cases where the prohibition order has been made in respect of the business itself, the enforcement authority must issue the certificate within three days of their being satisfied that the health risk condition is no longer fulfilled. If the proprietor has applied for such a certificate, the authority must determine, as soon as is reasonably practicable and in any event within 14 days, whether or not they are satisfied; and if they determine they are not satisfied, notify the proprietor of their reasons (s 11(7)). The certificate must be in the form prescribed by the Food Safety (Improvement and Prohibition – Prescribed Forms) Regulations 1991 (reproduced in Appendix 2).

A prohibition order preventing the proprietor or manager from participating in any food business can only be lifted by direction of the court (s 11(6)(b)). An application to the court to have the order lifted cannot be made before six months after the order was made or within three months after any previous application made by the proprietor or manager (s 11(8)). In considering lifting the order, the court must have regard to all the circumstances of the case, in particular the conduct of the proprietor or manager since the order was made.

Appeals

Section 37(1)(b) allows an appeal to the Magistrates' Court by way of complaint against the refusal to issue a certificate under s 11(6). The period for appealing is one month from the date on which notice of the decision was served on the appellant (s 37(5)(a)). A further appeal may be made to the Crown Court by a person aggrieved by the dismissal by a Magistrates' Court of his appeal (s 38(b)). An appeal also lies to the Crown Court against a magistrates' decision to make a prohibition order. The local authority has no right to appeal to the Crown Court where magistrates refuse to make an order.

Application to the manager of a food business

The prohibition provisions above apply to a manager of a food business in the same way as they apply to the proprietor of such a business; and any relevant statutory reference to the proprietor of the business is deemed to include a reference to the manager (s 11(10)). Manager, in relation to a food business, means any person who is entrusted by the proprietor with the day to day running of the business, or any part of it (s 11(11)).

Emergency prohibition notices

The powers of an authorised officer to serve an emergency prohibition notice (for which there is a form prescribed by the Food Safety (Improvement and Prohibition – Prescribed Forms) Regulations 1991 (reproduced in Appendix 2)) and to apply to a court for an emergency prohibition order in situations and circumstances where there is imminent risk of injury to health was an important inclusion in the FSA. This power is contained in s 12 and was introduced to cover potentially high-risk situations, eg where there may be gross contamination of premises due to flooding with sewage, serious infestation by rodents or where the risk of food contamination is excessive. The service of an emergency prohibition notice ensures the immediate closure of premises or immediate prevention of use of an item of equipment or the operation of a particular process. Once the notice has been served, the authorised officer must then apply to the court for an emergency prohibition order within three days. An emergency prohibition order cannot be made against a person. There is no right of appeal against an Emergency Prohibition Notice. Detailed procedures are set out in *Code of Practice No 6: Prohibition Procedures.*

Service of emergency prohibition notice

If an authorised officer of an enforcement authority is satisfied the health risk condition is fulfilled with respect to any food business, he may by notice served on the proprietor of the business (in the FSA referred to as an emergency prohibition notice) impose the appropriate prohibition (s 12(1)). Satisfaction as to the fulfilment of the health risk condition is, of course, based on a subjective judgment by the authorised officer at a particular time. The health risk condition is that set out in s 11(2) as amended by s 12(4), ie the risk must be imminent (see discussion later in this chapter).

As soon as practicable after the service of an emergency prohibition notice, the enforcement authority must fix the notice in an appropriately conspicuous position on the business premises and any person who knowingly contravenes the notice will be guilty of an offence (s 12(5)). *Code of Practice No 6* recommends that the authorised officer should if possible firmly fix the document inside the premises but in a position where it can clearly be seen and read by members of the public from the outside. A preferable position would be on the inside of the glass of a front display window (para 67). The enforcement authority can request the court making the prohibition order to make an ancillary order that the order should not be removed or defaced (see s 63 of the Magistrates' Courts Act 1980 – ancillary orders). If the ancillary order is breached, the authority may start proceedings under s 63(3) of the Magistrates' Courts Act 1980 for breach of the order (see paras 71–74 of the Code). No ancillary order is necessary in Scotland as it is an offence under s 78 of the Criminal Justice (Scotland) Act 1980 to damage another person's property without justifiable cause. If a notice is damaged, the matter should be reported to the Procurator Fiscal who can take action (para 75 of *Code of Practice No 6*). Any notice which has been damaged or removed should be replaced.

Cessation of an emergency prohibition notice

An emergency prohibition notice will cease to have effect:
  (a) if no application for an emergency prohibition order is made
      within the period of three days beginning with the service of
      the notice, at the end of that period; or
  (b) if such an application is so made, on the determination or
      abandonment of the application (s 12(7)).

Coventry City Council v Tee, 26 October 1992 (unreported) held
that 'application' in s 12(7)(a) refers to the Notice of Intention to
Apply for an Emergency Prohibition Order, but in s 12(7)(b) the
use of the word 'determination' denotes that 'application' in the
same subsection refers to the actual hearing.

Both an emergency prohibition notice and an emergency
prohibition order cease to have effect on the issue by the enforcement authority of a certificate that they are satisfied that
the proprietor has taken sufficient measures to secure that
the business no longer fulfils the health risk condition (s 12(9)).
The enforcement authority must issue a certificate under s 12(8)
(Certificate That There Is No Longer A Risk To Health for
which there is a form prescribed by the Food Safety (Improvement and Prohibition – Prescribed Forms) Regulations 1991
(reproduced in Appendix 2)) within three days of their being
satisfied. If the proprietor applies for such a certificate, the authority must determine, as soon as is reasonably practicable, and
in any event within 14 days, whether or not they are satisfied
and, if they determine they are not satisfied, notify the proprietor
why. If dissatisfied, a Notification of the Continuing Risk to
Health (see the forms prescribed by the Food Safety (Improvement
and Prohibition – Prescribed Forms) Regulations 1991 (reproduced
in Appendix 2)) must state the reasons for the authority's dissatis-
faction.

Compensation for losses suffered

Where an emergency prohibition notice is served on the proprietor
of a food business, the enforcement authority must compensate
him in respect of any loss suffered because he has complied with
the notice unless:
  (a) the enforcement authority makes an application for an
      emergency prohibition order within a period of three days
      beginning with the service of the notice; and

(b) the court declares itself satisfied, on the hearing of the application, that the health risk condition was fulfilled with respect to the business when the notice was served.

Any disputed question as to the right to or the amount of any compensation payable must be determined by arbitration or, in Scotland, by a single arbiter appointed, failing agreement by the parties, by the sheriff (s 12(10)).

In *Coventry City Council v Tee*, the court overruled the decision of the magistrates that the words 'application for an emergency prohibition order' in s 12(10)(a) referred to the hearing of that application rather than to the time at which the clerk to the justices was notified of the intention of the applicant to seek an order. The meaning of 'application' in s 12(10)(a) had to be determined by general considerations rather than determining its meaning in other subsections of s 12. In s 12(10)(a), it meant the process which will lead to a hearing beginning with the service of the Notice of Intention to Apply for an Emergency Prohibition Order, not the actual hearing. So there was compliance with the terms of s 12(10)(a) where the notice was served on 12 June 1991, the application by way of complaint was made to the court on 14 June 1991 and the hearing took place on 17 June 1991.

Supplementary provisions

Paragraphs 94–97 of *Code of Practice No 6* supplement the statutory compensation provisions of s 12(10). Compensation is payable in respect of any loss which is directly attributable to the wrongful service of the notice. The authority may assess the amount of compensation due taking into account (among other things) the following aspects where applicable: the length of time the business was affected; loss of trade, goodwill and wages; value of spoilt food; how much of the damage to trade is reparable and the proprietor's obligation to mitigate his own loss.

Alternatively, if the proprietor of the business agrees, a loss adjuster may be called in.

If there is disagreement between the proprietor and the food authority concerning the amount of compensation, then the food authority should seek to resolve this informally by arranging a meeting with the proprietor. If they cannot agree, arbitration should be applied for. Both the authority and the proprietor have the right to refer the matter to arbitration. In Scotland, the sheriff may appoint a single independent arbiter to resolve disputes over the right to or value of compensation. In England, the procedure is governed by the Arbitration Acts.

Emergency prohibition orders

Where a Magistrates' Court or, in Scotland, the sheriff, is satisfied, on the application by way of complaint of an authorised officer to the Magistrates' Court under ss 53–57 of the Magistrates' Courts Act 1980, that the health risk condition is fulfilled (see ss 11(2) and 12(4) of the FSA) with respect to any food business, the court or sheriff must, by emergency prohibition order, impose the appropriate prohibition (s 12(2)).

The authorised officer must not apply for an emergency prohibition order unless, at least one day before the date of the application, he has served notice of his application on the proprietor of the business of his intention to apply for the order (s 12(3)). The notice of application must be in the form prescribed by the Food Safety (Improvement and Prohibition – Prescribed Forms) Regulations 1991 (reproduced in Appendix 2).

Section 11(2) and (3) apply for the purposes of s 12 as they apply for the purposes of s 11, but as if the reference in subs (2) to risk of injury to health were a reference to imminent risk of such injury (s 12(4)).

Service

As soon as practicable after an emergency prohibition order has been made by the court, the enforcement authority must serve on the proprietor of the business a copy of the order and must fix a copy in an appropriately conspicuous position on the premises (s 12(6)). Any person who knowingly contravenes the order commits an offence. As with an emergency prohibition notice (see above) *Code of Practice No 6* recommends that the document should be fixed inside the premises but clearly visible from outside (para 67).

Prohibition procedures – Risk and imminent risk of injury to health

Section 11 applies if there is a risk of injury to health. Section 12, by contrast, applies if such a risk is imminent. In applying for an emergency prohibition order, and prior to serving an emergency prohibition notice, the authorised officer must be very certain that the risk is truly 'imminent', eg that an outbreak of food poisoning could result if action is not taken immediately. Authorised officers must, at all times, bear in mind the risk of a claim for compensation arising before exercising these draconian powers. On this basis, *Code of Practice No 6* provides guidance with regard to possible prohibition action.

Consideration of prohibition action

Guidance in the *Code of Practice No 6* lists a series of situations involving conditions where prohibition of premises, equipment and processes may be appropriate.

Prohibition of premises
Prohibition of premises may be appropriate when the following conditions are present:

(a) Serious infestations by birds, rats, mice, cockroaches or other vermin or a combination of these infestations resulting in actual food contamination or a real risk of food contamination (example of breach of health risk condition (s 11(2)(c)).

(b) Very poor structural condition and poor equipment and/or poor maintenance of routine cleaning and/or serious accumulation of refuse, filth or other extraneous matter resulting in a real risk of food contamination (example of breach of health risk condition (s 11(2)(b) and (c)).

(c) Serious drainage defects or flooding of the premises leading to actual contamination or a real risk of food contamination (example of breach of health risk condition (s 11(2)(c)).

(d) Premises or practices which seriously contravene the Food Safety (General Food Hygiene) Regulations 1995 and have been the cause of, or are involved with, an outbreak of food poisoning (example of breach of health risk condition (s 11(2)(c)).

Any combination of the above situations or the cumulative effect of contraventions which together represent an imminent risk of injury to health may justify a prohibition of premises.

Prohibition of equipment
The prohibition of equipment may be appropriate where, in addition to the above, the following circumstances are in existence:

(a) Use of defective equipment, eg a pasteuriser incapable of achieving the required pasteurisation temperature (example of breach of health risk condition (s 11(2)(c)).

(b) Use of equipment involving high-risk foods which has been inadequately cleaned or disinfected or which is obviously grossly contaminated and can no longer be properly cleaned (example of breach of health risk condition (s 11(2)(c)).

Prohibition of a process

Prohibition of a process may be appropriate where, in addition to the conditions for prohibition of premises, there is:

(a) Serious risk of cross contamination (example of breach of health risk condition (s 11(2)(b) or (c)).

(b) Inadequate temperature control, eg failure to achieve sufficiently high cooking temperatures (example of breach of health risk condition (s 11(2)(a)).

(c) Operation outside critical control criteria, eg incorrect pH of a product which might allow clostridium botulinum to multiply (example of breach of health risk condition (s 11(2)(a)).

(d) The use of a process for a product which is inappropriate (example of breach of health risk condition (s 11(2)(a)).

Seeking additional advice

Food authorities are encouraged to consider the use of outside experts where the process or treatment under consideration involves specialist knowledge or qualification.

Voluntary procedures

In certain situations, the owner of a food business may offer to close on a voluntary basis. Most food authorities are prepared to accept such an offer, in which case *Code of Practice No 6* recommends that the officer should:

(a) consider whether there is any risk of the premises being reopened without his knowledge and/or agreement;

(b) recognise that there is no legal sanction against a proprietor who reopens for business after offering to close; and

(c) explain to the proprietor that, by making the offer to close, he is relinquishing rights to compensation if a court subsequently declines to make a prohibition order.

The code recommends that, where an authorised officer accepts an offer to close voluntarily, he should obtain written confirmation of the proprietor's offer to close and an undertaking not to reopen without specific permission. Also, he should make frequent checks on the premises to ascertain that they have not reopened. The person giving any such undertaking should have authority to take such action.

Issuing the prohibition notice or order

Procedures for issuing emergency prohibition notices and prohibition orders are similar to those for improvement notices in terms of qualifications of authorised officers, the competence of such persons, service of notices and orders by authorised competent persons, actual procedures for service etc which allow reasonable flexibility in food authority activities.

Paragraph 37 of *Code of Practice No 6* recommends that the authorised officer should make every effort to serve a prohibition order, an emergency prohibition order or an emergency prohibition notice by delivering it to the proprietor of the business by hand or, in his absence, the manager. Where such service is not possible it should be served by post, with proof of delivery being obtained. The authorised officer should consult with the local justices' clerk to see if it would be possible to serve the order on the proprietor before he leaves the court. If the business is operated as a partnership every effort must be made to serve the notice or order on each and every one of the partners.

Application to the court

Most food authorities have well-established systems of liaison between authorised officers and the local justices' clerk. *Code of Practice No 6* recommends that, where such an arrangement does not exist, the authority should discuss a detailed programme of formal action with its litigation solicitor and with the justices' clerk with a view to clarifying details of local court practice to try and resolve potential difficulties in obtaining court time at short notice. It is essential, for instance, that a proprietor is notified that the authorised officer intends to apply for an emergency prohibition order and is aware of his rights.

Action to be taken prior to hearing

Paragraphs 48–49 of *Code of Practice No 6* set out the procedures the authorised officer should follow before the court hearing. He should organise periodic monitoring of the premises between service of a notice and the court hearing. This is particularly important if there is likely to be a delay. The monitoring need not be carried out by the authorised officer who initiated the action or served the notice. The premises should be re-inspected shortly before the hearing (preferably the day before or on the day of the hearing itself) by the original authorised officer, if this is possible, or by an authorised officer with the relevant experience. As corroborative evidence is required in Scotland, two officers should undertake the re-inspection. This should also be the case if any contravention was found during the period of monitoring. During a re-inspection the authorised officer should take particular note of any changes which have taken place since the notice was served.

Evidence required

Authorised officers are required to collect sufficient evidence to produce to the court in order to substantiate any enforcement proceedings (para 50 of the *Code of Practice No 6*). Evidence may include sketches and photographs, the latter taken with a polaroid camera, or a camera which prints the date the photograph was taken on the photograph. Samples may also be taken and produced in court, eg insects, dirt or other contaminants. Detailed contemporaneous notes should be taken recording what is observed during the inspection.

Procedures

Paragraph 53 of *Code of Practice No 6* instructs authorised officers about when to request the court to make a prohibition order. Following a second or subsequent inspection of premises prior to a court hearing for an offence under the processing or hygiene regulations listed in the Schedule to the code, an authorised officer may discover that the defect giving rise to the prosecution either has not been removed, or has been removed but has recurred because of a managerial lapse. If the proprietor of the food business is convicted by the court, the authorised officer should bring the attention of the court to s 11(1) in order for the court to consider a prohibition order on the premises, process or equipment. This ensures that, until the required action is taken, there is no risk to health.

The authorised officer should make every effort to inform the proprietor or manager of a food business or his legal representative before the hearing of the intention to draw the attention of the court to provisions relating to prohibition, either by serving written notice of the intention or, if that is not practicable, orally. Any evidence available to the food authority should be disclosed to the proprietor or his legal representative before the hearing (para 54 of the Code). If this does not happen, the defence solicitor should bring the matter to the attention of the court. The court is not obliged to adjourn the hearing for the evidence to be considered by the defence because the code is not statutorily binding and this recommendation is not a part to which officers must 'have regard'.

Appeals

There is no right of appeal against the decision of an authorised officer to serve an emergency prohibition notice, but that decision may be reviewable because of the compensation provisions of s 12(10), in particular the requirement that application for an emergency prohibition order be made within three days of the service of the emergency prohibition notice (see *Coventry City Council v Tee* 26 October 1992 (unreported)). However, there is a right of appeal to a Magistrates' Court, by way of complaint, against the refusal of the authority to issue a Certificate of Satisfaction under s 12(8) (s 37(1)(b)). The time limit for appealing against the refusal of the authority to issue a Certificate that there is no longer a risk to health is one month from the date on which notice of that decision was given to the appellant (s 37(5)(a)). Where the magistrates refuse to allow the appeal, the appellant has the right to appeal to the Crown Court (s 38(a)).

There is also a right of appeal to the Crown Court against a decision by magistrates to make an emergency prohibition order (s 38(b)).

Emergency control orders and ministerial directions

The power of the minister to make an emergency control order under s 13(1) has not, so far, been exercised. Section 13(1) was largely introduced to enable the minister to deal with adverse situations which were either so widespread geographically or so serious that they should be handled on a central government rather than a local food authority basis. The minister may also give directions under s 13(5) in certain situations. The powers are complementary to those of Part I of the Food and Environment Protection Act 1985, as amended by s 51 of the FSA, which are invoked following chemical or nuclear contamination of food over a very wide area.

Situations where these powers could be invoked are where there is strong evidence of an imminent risk to health from a food product distributed nationally and where the proprietors of the food business have refused to remove and recall the product, or where imported food may have subsequently been found to be contaminated with chemicals or failed to meet the food safety requirements.

Emergency control orders

If it appears to the minister that carrying out commercial operations in connection with food, food sources or contact materials of any class or description involves or may involve imminent risk of injury to health, he may, by emergency control order, prohibit such operations (s 13(1)). (See Chapter 2 for the meaning of 'commercial operation', 'food', 'food source' and 'contact material', and to the discussion of ss 11 and 12 for the meaning of 'imminent risk to health'.)

Any person who knowingly contravenes an emergency control order is guilty of an offence (s 13(2)). Under s 35, the offence is triable either way, with a £5,000 maximum penalty in a Magistrates' Court and/or imprisonment for not more than six months and an unlimited fine and/or two years' imprisonment in the Crown Court. The minister may consent, either unconditionally or subject to any condition that he consider appropriate, to the doing in a particular case of anything prohibited by an emergency control order (s 13(3)).

Defences available
It is a defence for a person charged with the offence of knowingly contravening an emergency control order under subs (2) to show:
  (a) that the minister gave his consent under s 13(3) to the contravention of the emergency control order; and

(b) that any condition subject to which that consent was given was complied with.

Ministerial directions

Under s 13(5)(a) the minister may give directions which appear to be necessary or expedient for the purpose of preventing the carrying out of commercial operations in connection with any food, food sources or contact materials to which an emergency control order applies. The minister must have reasonable grounds for believing that the emergency control order applies to the particular food, food source or contact material. Section 13(5)(b) gives the minister a sweeping power to do anything which appears to him to be necessary or expedient for the purpose of preventing the particular commercial operation.

Any person failing to comply with a direction given under s 13(5) is guilty of an offence (s 13(6)).

Power of the minister to recover expenses

If the minister does anything under this section in consequence of any person failing to comply with an emergency control order or a direction under this section, he may recover from that person any consequent expenses reasonably incurred (s 13(7)).

The food hazard warning system

The Department of Health, Ministry of Agriculture, Fisheries and Food, Scottish Office and Welsh Office operate a system to alert the public and food authorities to national or regional potential problems concerning food which does not meet food safety requirements.

Code of Practice No 16: Enforcement of the Food Safety Act 1990 in Relation to the Food Hazard Warning System deals with the operation of this system, which covers the use of voluntary surrender procedures, information received locally which may indicate a national emergency, action to be taken where a problem is identified by analysis or examination of samples, notification to central government departments, central government action, categories of notifications, malicious contamination of food and media relations.

Sampling and analysis

The duties of food authorities to appoint public analysts (s 27) and to provide facilities for examinations are discussed in Chapter 6. Sections 29, 30 and 31 deal with the procurement of samples, their analysis and procedures to regulate sampling and analysis. *Code of Practice No 7: Sampling for Analysis or Examination* provides enforcement guidance on the use of these powers.

Procurement of samples

Section 29 gives an authorised officer of an enforcement authority wide powers to procure samples of food, food sources and contact materials. He may purchase samples of any food, or any substance capable of being used in the preparation of food. He may also take a sample of any food or any substance, which appears to him to be intended for sale, or to have been sold, for human consumption; or which he finds on or in any premises which he is authorised to enter under s 32.

He also has power to take a sample from any food source, or a sample of any contact material which he finds on or in any such premises hc is authorised to enter under s 32.

Section 29(d) gives the authorised officer power to take a sample of any article or substance which he finds on or in any premises he is authorised to enter under s 32 and which he has reason to believe may be required as evidence in proceedings under the Act or relevant regulations.

Agents taking samples

Purchase or taking samples may be carried out by an agent of an authorised officer (*Stace v Smith* (1880) 45 JP 141; *Garforth v Esam* (1892) 56 JP 521; *Farley v Higginbotham* (1898) 42 SJ 309; *Tyler v Dairy Supply Co Ltd* (1908) 98 LT 867).

Food samples obtained by members of the public

A sample of food obtained and given by a member of the public to the authorised officer is not a 'sample' within the meaning of s 29 because that section requires the officer to 'purchase' or 'take' the sample (see *Arun District Council v Argyle Stores Ltd* (1986) *The Times*, 17 June). Section 29, therefore, does not apply to samples investigated by the enforcement authority after a complaint from a member of the public. Reference should be made to *Code of Practice No 2: Legal Matters* which informs officers that complaint samples should be properly stored and handled.

Regulation 6 of the Food Safety (Sampling and Qualifications) Regulations 1990 (SI 1990 No 2463) lays down three procedures to be followed by food authorities with regard to sampling for analysis. A sample should be divided into three parts and each part should be put into a sealed container. Each container should be marked. One container should be given to the owner of the sample giving him notice that it will be analysed. The second portion should be sent for analysis. The third portion should be retained (reg 6(1)). Where the sample consists of a sealed container, eg tin cans, and opening them might impede proper analysis, the officer may divide the containers into three lots and treat each lot as a separate part and carry out the same procedure as above (reg 6(2)). Where the sample cannot be divided into parts, the sample should be submitted for analysis and the owner given notice accordingly (reg 6(4)).

The purpose of retaining a third sample is to enable it to be submitted for analysis by the Government Chemist if a court so orders or if the authorised officer and owner agree.

Sampling for examination is dealt with in reg 8. Here the sample must be placed in a marked sealed container and submitted for examination having given notice of the examination to the owner. Failure to take into account all the procedural aspects of taking and analysing/examining a sample could result in acquittal in a case involving suspect food.

Proceedings cannot be taken in respect of only part of a sample taken or purchased. The sample must be co-extensive with the subject matter of the charge or a representative sample of some larger entity to which the charge relates. In *Skeate v Moore* [1972] 1 WLR 110 an officer took a sample of six meat pies from a baker's premises. The pies were divided into three pairs, and one pair of pies was sent for analysis. The baker was subsequently prosecuted for selling a pie which failed to comply with regulations covering the meat content for certain products. The baker's conviction was quashed by the Court of Appeal as there could not be a prosecution relating to one meat pie when a number of pies had been taken as the formal statutory sample.

Under reg 6(4) of the Food Safety (Sampling and Qualifications) Regulations 1990 it may now be possible only to purchase one meat pie for analysis because, if the authorised officer's opinion is that it is not reasonably practicable to divide the sample into three, he is not required to divide the sample as long as he gives notice to the owner that he intends to have analysed what he has taken.

Analysis of samples

Section 30 provides for the submission of samples by an authorised officer for either analysis by a public analyst or examination by a food examiner (s 30(1)). A person, other than such an officer, may also submit samples for analysis or examination (s 30(2)). Analysts and examiners must analyse or examine a sample as soon as practicable (s 30(5)) and must also give to the person by whom it is submitted a certificate signed by him specifying the result of the analysis or examination (s 30(6) and (7)). The certificate must be in the form prescribed by the Food Safety (Sampling and Qualifications) Regulations 1990 (reproduced in Appendix 2).

Where charged with an offence under the FSA, the production by one of the parties of a document purporting to be a certificate given by a food analyst or examiner or a document supplied to him by the other party as being a copy of such a certificate, is sufficient evidence of the facts stated in it unless, in the first case, the other party requires that the food analyst or examiner shall be called as a witness (s 30(8)).

Regulation of sampling and analysis

The ministers have power to make regulations supplementing the sampling and analysis provisions of s 30 (s 31). The provisions of s 30 have been supplemented by the Food Safety (Sampling and Qualifications) Regulations 1990.

The regulations seek to ensure that enforcement officers follow the proper procedures when handling samples which could be the basis of court proceedings. Guidance is provided in *Code of Practice No 7: Sampling for Analysis or Examination*. All samples which may result in legal proceedings if an adverse report is received following analysis or examination should be obtained in accordance with the procedures set out in the Code.

The Code covers the need for training of authorised officers in the appropriate techniques, procurement of samples, submission of certificates by food analysts or food examiners, and procedures covering the size and nature of samples for analysis, division of samples, containers for samples, transport and storage of samples and the notifications necessary to manufacturers, packers and importers of food.

Challenging a sample

Authorised officers must comply with the requirements of the above regulations. If they do not, the sample is invalid and the prosecution should be dismissed. The provisions of the Code are designed to supplement the regulations, but authorised officers only have to 'have regard' to the provisions of the Code which are in bold type (s 40 of the Act). Failure by the officer to comply with the Code should be brought to the attention of the court but the court is not obliged to dismiss the prosecution because of such failure. Evidence of such failures can be brought to the attention of the court to support a submission that the failures so prejudice the prosecution's case that it should be dismissed.

To challenge the validity of a sample taken for analysis or examination by an authorised officer, it must be proved beyond all reasonable doubt that one or more of the procedures detailed in the Code were not followed by the food authority and its officers. This could be shown if the sample was of insufficient size or quantity; unrepresentative of the batch in question; incorrectly marked/identified; incorrectly handled, contained, transported or stored; if the food authority failed to notify the manufacturer, packer or importer concerned, and if there was a substantial time delay between the taking of the sample and its analysis or examination.

Chapter 9

Avoiding Problems: Advising on Food Safety Issues

Introduction

This chapter examines the practical issues the lawyer may need to consider when requested by a client in the food sector to advise on the business systems which can facilitate compliance with food safety legislation. Implementation of proper management systems tailored to the needs of the individual business can prevent or minimise breaches of legislation. Those systems can also be vital in establishing to the satisfaction of a court the principal statutory defence in food safety legislation, due diligence.

The starting point for the lawyer advising on these matters is to gain an understanding of the client's operation. Broadly, the food industry can be split into a number of groups – manufacturers, wholesalers, importers, distributors, retailers and caterers. Some larger organisations may incorporate two or more of these groups. Each of these groups has different approaches, systems and problems in complying with food safety law, particularly with regard to their products, their procedures and the premises in which they operate their food business. Moreover, the last twenty-five years have seen the development of major food manufacturing, retailing and catering concerns, whose needs are far removed from those of the small family-run business.

The food distribution chain

Manufacturers must ensure that raw materials and processing operations produce a substance which meets established compositional and bacteriological requirements, and that the food premises and processes comply with current hygiene and temperature control requirements. Certain food manufacturers produce 'own label' products for the national supermarket chains. Not only do they need to meet current legal requirements, but they must also satisfy the very stringent preparation, production, bacteriological, compositional, packaging and labelling specifications laid down by these organisations in the contract governing the business relationship.

Wholesalers, on the other hand, are concerned with bulk storage, the breaking of bulk and ensuring the integrity of the product in all respects before it passes to a distributor and onwards to the retailer or caterer.

Importers have the duty to ensure the products they import meet current European and UK standards with regard to composition, purity, labelling and packaging.

Distributors, who may be independent companies or part of a manufacturing chain, need to ensure rapid delivery of particularly high-risk products, at the correct temperature and, in many cases, using temperature-controlled vehicles.

Retailers, at the end of the distribution chain, must ensure the product is fit for human consumption at the point of sale and is stored under hygienic conditions and at the correct temperature.

Perhaps the most difficult business operation is that of running a catering business. This involves the reception and storage of raw materials, the cooking and preparation of food under hygienic conditions and its eventual presentation to the customer. The range and scale of catering businesses is enormous, from hotels, restaurants and cafes to take-away operations and sandwich bars.

Understanding the business activity

Each of these groups in the food distribution chain can breach food safety law and it is essential that lawyers have a good grasp of the principal problems and current measures taken by individual companies and proprietors of food businesses to eliminate or control these problems. This requires a broad understanding of the business processes and operations of the food safety management systems that need to be operated in order to comply with the general requirements of the law and more specific requirements applicable to particular processes or industries.

What food safety legislation applies to the business?

The first question to address is what general and specific legislation applies to the business under consideration. The Food Safety Act

1990, the Food Safety (General Food Hygiene) Regulations 1995 and the Food Safety (Temperature Control) Regulations 1995 apply to most food businesses. However, the more specialised type of food business can be subject to specific regulatory requirements either in addition to, or instead of, these general requirements, such as those relating to ice-cream, milk, liquid egg, quick-frozen foodstuffs, slaughterhouses, the meat and fish industries and businesses which irradiate food.

Certain health and safety-related legislation, such as the Workplace (Health, Safety and Welfare) Regulations 1992 (SI No 3004) and the Control of Substances Hazardous to Health Regulations 1994 (SI No 3246) may also impinge on the requirements relating to the safety of food products and catering operations. It is important for the lawyer to adopt an integrated approach when advising on a food safety issue to avoid conflict with duties under other applicable legislation. For example, reg 5 of the Workplace (Health, Safety and Welfare) Regulations 1992 places an absolute duty on employers to maintain (including cleaning as appropriate) the workplace and the equipment, devices and systems in an efficient state, in efficient working order and in good repair. The Food Safety (General Food Hygiene) Regulations 1995 place upon proprietors of the food business many obligations concerning the state of the premises of the business which interrelate with this duty (see Chapter 4).

Due diligence and compliance

Chapter 5 (pp 80–81) contains details of the legal requirements which are necessary to establish the principal defence under the FSA and regulations made under or continued in force by it: 'due diligence'. Section 21 of the FSA requires that the defendant prove that he took all reasonable precautions *and* exercised all due diligence to avoid the commission of the offence by himself or by a person under his control. These are cumulative matters, not alternatives. Any person relying on this defence must be able to show that he has taken positive action to prevent the alleged offence from being committed. Moreover, taking reasonable precautions involves setting up systems of control having regard to the nature of the risk involved, whilst due diligence involves securing the proper operation of that system.

Modern protective legislation, particularly in the areas of occupational health and safety and food safety, places considerable emphasis on the need for risk assessment. The business which implements measures either to prevent or control exposure to risks is more likely to establish a 'due diligence' defence to the satisfaction of a court. Although the phrase 'risk assessment' is not used in food legislation, it is indirectly part of food law by virtue of the legal obligation on food business proprietors to identify steps in the activities of the food business which are critical to ensuring food safety and to ensure that adequate safety procedures are identified, implemented, maintained and reviewed (reg 4(3) of the Food Safety (General Food Hygiene) Regulations 1995 – see Chapter 4).

It is also part of enforcement practice since *Code of Practice No 9: Food Hygiene Inspections* (revised September 1995) emphasises the importance of systematic hazard analysis both by food businesses in their day-to-day operation and by enforcement officers when undertaking inspections. Such analysis is significant in ensuring compliance with the 'food safety requirements' under the FSA.

However, food businesses are not legally required to adopt a specific system for identifying the steps which are critical for ensuring food safety, such as Hazard Analysis Critical Control Points or Assured Safe Catering. Enforcement officers therefore do not have the power to require implementation of these systems. On the other hand, enforcement officers are advised to encourage use of such systems on a purely voluntary basis.

The Code recommends that when inspecting a food business, enforcement officers should take account not only of whether a formal hazard analysis system has been adopted but whether it is being operated effectively, with proper identification and monitoring of critical control points and appropriate corrective action where necessary. Moreover, whether or not the business has adopted a formal system, the enforcement officer should focus on identifiable hazards.

In certain high risk operations, such as large scale food manufacturing and processing, a formal management system aimed at ensuring food safety is essential.

Two risk assessment systems which are of particular significance in ensuring safe food production are the Hazard Analysis Critical Control Points System (HACCP) and Assured Safe Catering (ASC).

Hazard analysis critical control points system

HACCP as a system identifies specific biological, chemical and physical hazards that may adversely affect food safety and develops measures for their control.

The system incorporates a number of basic principles. It identifies the principal food hazards, the risks arising from these hazards and the likelihood or probability of their occurrence. It determines the points, procedures and operational steps that can be controlled to eliminate the hazard or minimise the likelihood of its occurrence – the Critical Control Points ('CCPs'). It establishes target levels and tolerances which must be met to ensure that the CCP is under control, a monitoring system to ensure control of the CCP by scheduled testing or observation; that corrective action will be taken when monitoring indicates that a particular CCP is not under control, procedures for verification, including supplementary tests and procedures to confirm that HACCP is working effectively and documentation concerning all procedures and records appropriate to the principles of HACCP and their application.

The various steps in the hazard system are shown in Fig 1 (opposite). The following definitions are associated with the HACCP system. A hazard is an unacceptable contamination of a biological, chemical or physical nature, and/or survival or multiplication of micro-organisms of concern to safety (or spoilage), and/or unacceptable production or persistence in foods of toxins or other undesirable products of microbial metabolism. Biological hazards include infectious or toxigenic bacteria (known as pathogens), rickettsia, viruses, moulds and parasites. Chemical hazards include pesticides, cleaning compounds, antibiotics, heavy metals and additives, such as sulphites and monosodium glutamate. Physical hazards include metal fragments, glass, wood, splinters and stones. Severity is the magnitude of the hazard or the degree of consequences that can result when a hazard exists. Three categories of disease-causing hazards are, first, life-threatening illnesses, secondly, severe or chronic illnesses and, thirdly, moderate or mild illnesses. Risk is an estimate of the probability of occurrence of a hazard or the sequential consequences of several hazards. A critical control point is an operation (practice, procedure, process or location) at which a preventive or control measure can be exercised that will eliminate, prevent or minimise the hazard. A control point is an operation at which preventive and/or control actions are taken because of good manufacturing practices, regulations, product reputation, corporate/company policies or aesthetics. This distinction between control points and critical control points is one of the unique aspects of the HACCP concept which sets out priorities on risk and emphasises operations that offer the greatest potential for control. Criteria are specified limits or characteristics of a physical, chemical or biological nature. Criteria must be specified for each critical control point.

Fig 1   The HACCP system

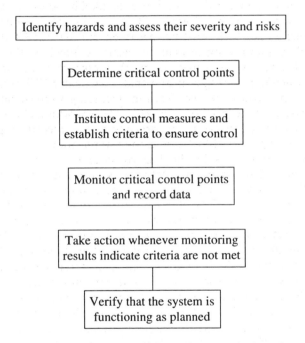

So, HACCP is a structured approach to analysing the potential hazards in an operation and estimating the risks arising from them, identifying the points in the operation where the hazards may occur and deciding which points are critical to consumer safety.

The advantages of the HACCP system are numerous. It is systematic as all potential hazards are identified; problems are foreseen and forestalled. It is efficient as it concentrates the control effort at the critical steps in the operation. By using checks which can be done cheaply, quickly and easily, such as measuring temperatures and visual assessment, it can be economical. Fast checks allow rapid response when action is needed. The process is controlled on the spot by the operator, not by a laboratory remote from the operation.

Implementing HACCP

The first step towards implementing HACCP is the formation of a HACCP team. The team may be large or small, depending upon the operation. It should be composed of people who know and understand the business's food products and their uses. The owner or employees of a business may have the necessary expertise themselves if they have had appropriate training in food hygiene, or they may have to seek advice from outside experts, such as microbiologists, especially if specialised processes such as vacuum packing or cook-chill are involved. A HACCP scheme is only as good as the people who draw it up.

The second step is to define the process operated by the business. The team draws up a flow chart of all aspects of the food operation from raw materials through processing to storage and consumer handling.

Thirdly, the team must identify the hazards and work out the CCPs. A hazard is anything that may harm the consumer and, as the definition above demonstrates, it can be of a chemical, biological or physical nature. The team identifies the potential hazards associated with the food at all stages from raw materials to processing, manufacture and distribution until the point of consumption. Then the team assesses the likelihood of occurrence of these hazards and it identifies the preventive measures necessary for their control. Finally the team identifies the steps that can be controlled to eliminate each hazard or minimise the likelihood of its occurring. These are the CCPs.

Fourthly, the team recommends monitoring and control procedures. For each CCP the team recommends what is to be done, when it is to be done and who is to do it. It also lays down the limits outside which further action, eg referral to management or external experts, is needed.

Fifthly, the team must ensure that the recommended monitoring and controls are actually carried out. This will include maintaining records of the HACCP process as well as the controls monitored at the CCP for each batch of food.

Finally, the design and operation of the HACCP should be reviewed whenever the food processing operation is altered, however slight the alteration may appear. The scheme should

be reviewed periodically even when there have been no altera-
tions. The frequency of review will depend on the degree of
risk from the operation. Reviews should be conducted, at least,
annually.

Assured safe catering

ASC can be seen as an extension to HACCP specifically directed at
the catering industry. It is a technique developed by the Campden
Food and Drink Research Association together with specialists
from the Ministry of Agriculture, Fisheries and Food and the
Department of Health.

As a system, ASC analyses the various food hazards that can
arise, and the controls necessary, at the various stages of catering
activities, eg dealing with raw materials, storage, preparation and
cooking.

Broadly, ASC incorporates the following stages: planning; establishment of procedures, including training; the development of a
flow diagram showing the various catering steps; analysing each
catering step; repeating the analysis to check it; system checking
and system reviewing. Analysis of each catering step involves the
following: listing the food hazards; identifying the control measures; identifying the critical control points; developing a checking
or recording system; putting the system into action and checking
the system.

The operation of ASC can assist caterers to comply with their
obligation under reg 4(3) of the Food Safety (General Food
Hygiene) Regulations 1995 to identify the steps in the activities of
the food business which are critical to ensuring food safety and to
ensure that adequate safety procedures are identified, implemented,
maintained and reviewed. As with HACCP, there is no specific
legal requirement to operate ASC. However, the proprietor of a
food business operating such a system would stand a greater
chance of proving that he had taken all reasonable precautions and
exercised all due diligence than one who was not operating the
system.

Due diligence systems, with particular emphasis on hazard
analysis, are becoming an increasingly significant feature of the
operation of food businesses in the UK. For the lawyer, a basic
knowledge of the theory of these systems is useful in two respects.
First, it can assist in analysing the merits of a due diligence defence.
Secondly, when advising on compliance issues generally, the lawyer

can adopt a proactive approach by making the client aware of such systems and how to implement them.

General food safety management systems

Whilst HACCP and ASC are techniques businesses may use to assist them in risk assessment, they are not a replacement for general management systems tailored to the needs of the particular food business. Lawyers are unlikely to be required to formulate management systems for their clients. However, where the lawyer is advising a client on compliance issues, a proper understanding of general management systems can assist in reviewing particular systems adopted by the client or in advising what matters the client should consider when formulating management systems. It can also assist in isolating gaps in the management system which may result in legal liability or difficulty in establishing a due diligence defence in the event of a prosecution for breach of food safety law.

Food safety management systems can be separated into pre-incident and post-incident strategies. An incident can be the outbreak of food poisoning affecting many people, which can have serious repercussions for a food manufacturer or catering organisation.

It is essential, therefore, that various pre-incident strategies be devised with a view to preventing such incidents arising in the first place. These can be classed as 'clean place' and 'clean person' strategies.

'Clean place' strategies are concerned with the structural, environmental and organisational aspects of food safety control and include clean premises, plant and equipment, processes, working environment and systems of work. Their aim is a reduction in the physical, chemical and biological conditions likely to lead to a food safety incident.

'Clean person' strategies are concerned with people, in particular, food handlers and include personal hygiene, the provision and proper use of personal protective equipment, selection and placement of staff, adequate supervision and control and competent and trained food handlers. Their aim is an increase in the subjective perception of food safety risks by food handlers generally.

Where an incident does arise, the business should implement the following 'post-incident' strategies. There should be a contingency plan covering the aftermath of a food safety incident, in particular reporting and recording procedures, liaison with the food authority enforcement officers and the Public Health Laboratory Service, submission of samples, bacteriological examination of surfaces, plant and equipment and health surveillance of staff.

An improvement strategy should be in place which is concerned with learning from the errors and omissions to prevent a recurrence of the food safety incident. It may include staff training, the implementation of supplier monitoring and product recall systems and the provision of information to staff aimed at raising their awareness of the causes of the incident.

A feedback strategy should be adopted to improve the performance of the business and to prevent recurrence of the incident. It should include the objective interpretation and use of statistical information and the identification of deficiencies in areas such as training, supervision, health surveillance and bacteriological control.

Management systems and procedures

It is essential that those representing defendants whose organisations operate HACCP and/or ASC have a good understanding of these systems and the management procedures necessary to implement them. However, proof of the existence of such systems and their implementation may be insufficient to meet the particular charge against a defendant. So, lawyers should discuss with clients whether any of the following general management systems are relevant to an alleged offence or, alternatively, when advising on compliance issues.

Food quality and safety policy

The intentions of the organisation can be formalised in a Statement of Food Quality and Safety Policy. This policy should incorporate a statement of intent and the arrangements for implementation of the policy. A director should be identified as having general responsibility for all food safety operations throughout the organisation.

Whilst the production of such a policy is not a legal requirement, it can be the first step in endeavouring to establish the due diligence defence. It can demonstrate to a court that the business has implemented the general principles laid down by the House of Lords in *Tesco Supermarkets v Nattrass* [1971] 2 All ER 127, which emphasised the importance of legal responsibility resting with the controlling mind of a company, the board of directors, which could delegate responsibility to a particular director or senior manager. A clear indication of the policy being put into practice and monitoring the achievement of its objectives is essential. The Policy Statement should clearly identify the individual responsibilities of staff at all levels. Detailed guidance on procedures and systems should be featured in a company Food Safety Manual, which should be referred to in the Policy Statement. Typical elements of a company Food Safety Manual are: the procedure for providing information, instruction, training and supervision; specific food contamination risks and the precautions to be taken by food handlers and other staff; procedures for corrective action; customer complaint procedures; details of registration under current regulations; management procedures to be followed in the event of enforcement action under the FSA and regulations; emergency procedures, including product recall arrangements; liaison arrangements with officers of the food authorities; cleaning and preventive maintenance arrangements; health surveillance procedures; infestation prevention and control procedures; hygiene monitoring arrangements and responsibilities; product labelling and coding systems; inspection procedures for raw materials, ingredients, packaging materials and intermediate products; waste storage and disposal arrangements and temperature control systems for high-risk products. Some of these elements are considered in detail below.

Monitoring systems
There should be a formal system for monitoring operations, including frequent inspections and audits of the premises, temperature control of the premises and product, bacteriological assay where appropriate, and a corrective action reporting system to ensure items for attention are dealt with as expeditiously as necessary. Such systems should ensure that the performance of contractors, such as contract cleaners and pest control contractors, is monitored on a regular basis.

Cleaning schedules
The main problem with cleaning operations is that, in many cases, responsibilities for the various cleaning activities are not clearly defined. A cleaning schedule should be prepared and operated. This document should incorporate the following elements: the area and item of plant, machinery and structure to be cleaned; the

materials to be used (the choice of the correct preparation for the type and degree of soiling is important and manufacturers' instructions should be followed closely); the equipment to be used; the method of cleaning (with adequate staff training to implement it); the frequency of cleaning should be specified, eg at the end of the shift, once per hour, at the end of the production run etc; any precautions needed (in certain cases, it may be necessary clearly to identify the hazards from the use of certain cleaning compounds or preparations and the precautions needed by operators to ensure appropriate safety measures: the requirements of the Control of Substances Hazardous to Health Regulations 1994 which apply to most detergent solutions) and identifying who is responsible for implementing each cleaning operation and ensuring its satisfactory completion.

A designated manager should have specific responsibility for monitoring compliance with the cleaning schedule on a regular basis. In many organisations, a hygiene officer undertakes this function.

Preventive maintenance
Every year the courts deal with complaints of foreign bodies in food. Many of these foreign bodies, nuts, bolts, pieces of string, wood, staples, etc, are caused by poor plant and structural maintenance.

A planned maintenance programme for plant, equipment, structural items and facilities is important to ensure compliance with the 'food safety requirements' of the FSA (see Chapter 3 pp 24–30) and the Rules of Hygiene of Sched 1 to the Food Safety (General Food Hygiene) Regulations 1995 (see Chapter 4 pp 47–9) and to prevent food safety incidents. Such incidents are a frequent cause of consumer complaints to food authorities, and the majority of food authorities tend to instigate prosecutions for foreign body offences. Planned maintenance programmes should take the form of detailed schedules and should incorporate the following features: the item of plant, identified in a Plant Register, structural feature to be maintained; the maintenance procedure, including specific methods of maintenance, the materials and equipment to be used and, for plant and equipment, the criteria for testing following the maintenance operation; the frequency of maintenance; any precautions necessary in the maintenance operation; and individual responsibility for ensuring that the maintenance operation takes place.

Regular monitoring to ensure correct implementation of the programme should be undertaken by a senior manager with corrective action being taken where necessary. It is vital that well-documented maintenance records are retained, first, to provide a record for the business and, secondly, to provide documentary evidence in court should it be necessary.

Infestation prevention and control
Evidence of infestation by crawling and flying insects, rodents and birds is one of the common features of prosecution under food safety legislation. All staff should receive basic training in the identification of the signs of infestation, with immediate reporting to a designated manager.

Infestation is a food hazard in that any form of infestation represents a serious risk of contamination to food. In many cases, it can render food unfit for human consumption. There is a general duty on the operator of a food business to ensure that the layout, design, construction and size of food premises permits good food hygiene practices, including avoiding cross contamination by external sources of contamination such as pests (Food Safety (General Food Hygiene) Regulations 1995 Sched 1 Ch I, para 2(c)).

The prevention and control of infestation by rodents, crawling and flying insects and birds is concerned with the following three specific strategies.

Structural proofing includes any measures aimed at preventing access to premises by the various types of infestation and the abolition, so far as possible, of harbourage areas where breeding can take place. Proofing measures include specific structural treatments to external doors, at the eaves of a building, between walls and structural claddings and at the junction of a floor and brick wall and screening of openable windows.

The second line of defence against infestation is proper hygiene and housekeeping procedures. The implementation of formally documented cleaning and housekeeping procedures should be directed at eliminating harbourage and the availability of food, water and shelter to pests.

In spite of structural proofing and hygiene measures, infestations may still occur. In such circumstances, eradication measures should be introduced immediately and should continue until eradication is completed. The measures taken must be appropriate to the particular situation. Eradication measures can be undertaken by trained staff in a company-operated pest control scheme or through the use of an external commercial pest control company. In some cases, local environmental health departments may provide such a service.

The operation of a company pest control scheme, namely utilising the services of trained staff working under the direction of a hygiene officer or hygiene supervisor, has much to commend it, provided that responsibility for such a scheme is clearly identified at senior management level. There must be a firm commitment by senior management to the initial cost of structural proofing, the maintenance of appropriate hygiene and housekeeping, with eradication measures as a third line of defence.

In most cases, however, the services of a commercial pest control company are utilised. To ensure effective performance from such organisations, it is essential that the terms of the contract of service are fully understood by management and that their performance is monitored on an on-going basis.

Temperature controls

There should be procedures for ensuring compliance with the requirements of the Food Safety (Temperature Control) Regulations 1995 which are considered in detail in Chapter 4.

Health surveillance

Health surveillance, namely the regular monitoring of the health of food handlers and other people who may come into contact with food, such as drivers, porters and cleaners, is an important feature of the prevention of food-borne disease associated with food products.

Health surveillance covers a broad range of activities directed at protecting the health of the food handler and the purity of the product. It is most effectively undertaken by occupational health nurses with support, where necessary, from an occupational physician who has a good understanding of the problems of the food industry. Their involvement is, however, only likely to be economically viable in larger businesses. Where resources do not allow the use of employed professionals, health surveillance should be provided by an external occupational health service.

Chapter VIII, para 2 of Sched 1 to the Food Safety (General Food Hygiene) Regulations 1995 requires staff who know or suspect that they are suffering or are likely to be suffering from, or are a carrier of, a disease likely to be transmitted through food or while afflicted with infected wounds, skin infections, sores or diarrhoea to be excluded from any food handling area in any capacity in which there is any likelihood of directly or indirectly contaminating food with pathogenic organisms.

Accordingly, some form of regular health surveillance is essential, together with a firm requirement for food handlers and others to report various diseases and conditions to management immediately and certainly prior to commencing work.

Forms of health surveillance

Health surveillance procedures in the food industry may include:
(a) the completion by those seeking employment of a, 'Pre-employment Health Screening Questionnaire', at the job application stage;
(b) pre-employment health examinations of all staff with a view to assessing their fitness to handle food;
(c) on-going health examinations, eg six monthly, annually, of all staff;
(d) health examination on return to work following prolonged illness or food-borne infection;
(e) examination of staff for the detection of specific conditions, such as dermatitis;
(f) counselling of staff on general health-related issues; and
(g) health supervision of specific groups, such as young persons and disabled persons.

Food safety training, information and instruction

The provision of information, instruction and training for all grades of staff is essential in order to meet the broad requirements of the FSA and also the training obligation of Ch X of Sched 1 to the Food Safety (General Food Hygiene) Regulations 1995 which requires proprietors of food businesses to ensure that food handlers are supervised and instructed and/or trained in food hygiene matters commensurate with their work activities (see Chapter 4 pp 60–1).

Food safety training should be directed at improving staff knowledge of the risks to food safety through poor handling techniques and personal hygiene practices. Training should endeavour to change attitudes, raise awareness, bring about pride in particular jobs and an appreciation of the individual's role in ensuring the production of both clean and safe products. A company policy on food safety training should be established indicating the responsibilities of training managers, personnel managers and others responsible for training, such as quality assurance managers and hygiene officers. Food safety training should be undertaken on induction, at the introduction of new products, change of job or work activity and on promotion.

Evidence of staff having received formal training may be crucial in mounting a due diligence defence. Formal training is offered through the basic, intermediate and advanced courses run under the auspices of the Chartered Institute of Environmental Health. Most local environmental health departments run these courses on a phased or in-company basis, together with Institute-approved training providers.

Consumer complaints procedure

One of the principal criticisms of both officers of food authorities and consumers is that food businesses do not handle complaints in a professional manner. People who complain about food products are frequently seen as 'troublemakers' or as those 'who want something for nothing'. In most cases, people who have taken the trouble to complain, which may entail some degree of inconvenience or the risk of an embarrassing 'scene', are the very ones who seek the support of the enforcement agencies if they do not get satisfaction from the food business.

Whilst the fines for individual offences under the FSA and regulations may not be prohibitive, cumulative fines for numerous offences can cost businesses a great deal of money. Furthermore, the adverse publicity following such cases can be damaging to an organisation's image in the marketplace. It is essential, therefore, that food businesses have a formal procedure for dealing with complaints from consumers, the principal objective of which is to ensure appropriate and consistent handling of all product-related complaints and incidents.

The initial stage of the procedure should be the immediate reporting of the incident through a senior manager to a manager responsible for quality assurance. Judgments as to the priority and appropriate action should be made only by the quality assurance manager and not by line managers. The importance of immediate reporting should be emphasised at all levels of the organisation.

Information relating to the complaint is best dealt with through the use of a product complaint form or record, which should detail the name of the person receiving the complaint; the name, address and telephone number of the complainant; the date and time of receipt of the complaint; nature of the complaint/incident; details of samples obtained or arrangements made to obtain samples; date of purchase of product; product type and brand name; product code number; product purchase location; product purchase date; 'best before' or 'use by' date; witnesses to the complaint/incident and action taken by the complainant.

Following receipt of the complaint, the quality assurance manager must assess its seriousness. Depending upon his judgment, different levels of the organisation will be involved and appropriate action taken. In certain situations it may be necessary to operate the company product recall procedure (see below) but, in the majority of cases, a quick response at local level, aimed at reassuring the complainant, may be sufficient.

Sometimes, a complainant may want to meet a company representative. Any meeting with a complainant should take place in the presence of a third party so that, if required, there is a witness who can give evidence about what was said at the meeting. The principal objective of such a meeting must be the examination of the food product involved with a view to identifying the reasons for the complaint and establishing the cause of the defect in the product.

Food authorities to whom complaints are reported often request a meeting with a company representative to discuss the complaint. The complaints procedure should address the company's approach to such a request. Often early co-operation with a food authority forestalls prosecution. The lawyer should advise the company on its obligation not to obstruct food authority officers in the execution of their duty since obstruction is an offence under s 33 of the FSA (see Chapter 7, pp 114–15).

No admissions of liability should be made to either the complainant or to a food authority officer. Many companies include in their procedure a provision that the complainant should be informed that a report will be sent to a senior manager and that a copy of the report will be sent to them in due course. The company should be given advice about the drafting and use of such reports. Reports should not contain any admission of liability or other damaging material. Providing a copy of the report to the consumer can be double-edged. It can be good for customer relations by demonstrating that the company has taken the complaint seriously and has acted on it. However, the complainant could provide a copy of the report to an investigating enforcement officer which could be used by him in court in the event of a prosecution. If the complainant commences civil proceedings against the company, the report would be discoverable unless it came into existence for the purpose of giving or getting legal advice or in relation to contemplated or existing legal proceedings.

Product recall

Serious incidents could result in product recall. How to recover the product from the marketplace quickly, quietly and efficiently, without attracting the attention of the media, is a subject which has been pursued by the food industry at great length over the last decade, largely as a result of various food sabotage incidents and national food safety scares. Again, there should be a formal product recall procedure, with an identified senior manager responsible for implementing the various levels of recall, both nationally and locally.

The lawyer should advise the client of the potential criminal and/or civil liability which may result either from a failure to recall product or from a delay in product recall. Any or all of the major offences under the FSA could be committed if a defective product is not withdrawn from the market. Where there is a failure to withdraw and the product causes harm or loss to a customer, that customer could have claims against the business in negligence, breach of contract and under the Consumer Protection Act 1987.

Ingredient and final product specification

Methods should be established to ensure compliance with specifications for raw materials and final products.

Liaison with enforcement officers

Every food business should have procedures for responding to matters arising from routine inspections of or enforcement action taken by food authorities. The responsibility for liaising with Environmental Health Officers (EHOs) should be clearly identified in the company's policy statement. Liaison may take place and may be maintained in a number of ways:

(a) by seeking guidance, particularly at the design stage of new projects;
(b) by discussing matters such as the formulation of cleaning schedules, preventive maintenance schedules, sampling procedures, temperature control systems, infestation control procedures, prior to their implementation;
(c) by agreeing food safety training needs for individual groups prior to running training programmes;
(d) by agreeing complaints procedures and product recall systems;
(e) by seeking agreement on the contents of food safety manuals and operating procedures prior to publication;
(f) by reviewing corrective action reporting procedures;
(g) by the introduction of formal systems, such as Hazard Analysis Critical Control Points (see pp 158–61).

The agreement of a local enforcement officer to company procedures cannot bind the food authority since such authorities cannot fetter their discretion to prosecute for breaches of duties which they are obliged by statute to enforce.

Contractors' activities

Most organisations have formal procedures to regulate the activities of contractors on site, whether main contractors extending the premises or contractors involved in activities such as window cleaning and electrical work. Whilst company contractors' regulations are largely concerned with ensuring appropriate levels of health and safety performance, many instances of food contamination can be associated with contractors' employees failing to recognise the significance of working on food premises. Procedures should concentrate on the briefing of contractors in the food safety requirements, physical segregation of specific areas in certain cases and control over all potential contamination-producing activities in the work.

Food safety specialists

A Food Safety Manual should identify the role, function and accountability of specialists, such as food technologists, hygiene officers and laboratory staff.

Contractual terms in management systems

There has been a marked change in the way food sector contracts are drafted since the passing of the FSA. Under s 102 of the Food Act 1984, a business had a defence to offences of selling, or offering, exposing, advertising or possessing for sale any food if it had a written warranty that it was lawful to sell the particular food. It was commonplace for supply contracts to include a warranty to the effect that product complied in all respects with the Food Act 1984 and all regulations made under or continued in force by it. The repeal of the Food Act 1984 swept away the warranty defence. Instead, the only defence to the principal offences under the FSA, is the s 21 due diligence defence. Nevertheless, having a warranty that food does comply with the Food Safety Act 1990 and all regulations made under or continued in force by it is still a worthwhile part of the armoury of the business when mounting the due diligence defence. It enables the business to demonstrate to a court that it imposed upon the other contractual party a contractual duty to ensure that food supplied to it complies with the law. A blanket warranty has little substance (see *Riley v Webb* (1987) 151 JP 372). The warranty clause should refer to the specific product by name or to products listed in a schedule to the contract or it can incorporate by reference another document which lists the products, such as a product specification. The supplier should also be required to warrant that it takes all reasonable precautions and exercises all due diligence to avoid the commission of offences by it or by persons under its control.

Chapter 5 discusses in detail what has become known as the 'deemed due diligence' defence. A deemed due diligence defence to charges under section 8, 14 and 15 of the FSA is available to any business which either sells branded goods (s 21(4)) or goods under its name or mark (s 21(3)). In summary, it enables a business to avoid liability for an offence committed by a person not under its control or where reliance has been placed on information supplied by that other person to the business. Such businesses should incorporate into their contracts with suppliers clauses which determine what information is to be supplied to them and the legal effect of a failure to supply any, or to supply defective, information. Where inspection of the supplier's premises will be a necessary part of the business relationship, the contract should specify the right of the business to inspect the premises and equipment of the supplier.

The contract should impose upon the supplier a contractual duty forthwith to notify the business of any, or any suspected, defect in the product.

From the point of view of civil liability, the supplier should be required to indemnify the business in respect of all losses arising from a breach of warranty. In addition, lawyers should consider the need to include in a contract a term dealing with civil liability arising from either the withdrawal of product from the market voluntarily or compulsorily through seizure of it by an authorised officer of a food authority in the exercise of his powers to do so under s 9(3)(b) of the FSA. Section 9 provides that food authorities can be required to compensate food businesses for the depreciation in the value of food resulting from action taken by an authorised officer. That provision may be insufficient to cover all recoverable losses suffered by the business and the contract should address whether the business has the right of recovery against the other contracting party.

External advisers

The lawyer has a role to play in providing advice to food sector clients about management systems. Without environmental health training, however, it is unlikely that the lawyer can draft in detail the systems the client may need to operate in the food business to prevent or minimise breaches of food safety law and to ensure best practice. Where the business does not employ environmental health officers who have the necessary training and skills to draft and implement management systems, the lawyer should consider with the client the use of external food safety consultants who can be employed on an independent contractor basis to set up the systems. If finance is not available to consult external advisers, the business should explore with the local food authority what assistance it can provide to the business. Many of the codes of practice which are designed to ensure that uniform enforcement methods are operated by food authorities stress that they are not just there to enforce the law but that they should also provide advice and assistance to businesses on compliance with legal requirements and on best practice.

Implementing management systems can be an expensive undertaking, particularly where it entails structural changes in the premises and/or the purchase of new equipment. Unless finance is unlimited, the business probably will have to prioritise how it spends scarce resources. It is important, therefore, that whoever does provide assistance distinguishes between what is necessary to ensure compliance with the law and what is just best practice.

Application of new legislation and standards

Food safety law is constantly changing particularly as a result of EU legislation. The following sources of information may prove useful for lawyers to keep abreast of food issues and evolving legislation.

Central government

The Department of Health, the Ministry of Agriculture, Fisheries and Food, the Scottish Office and the Welsh Office provide excellent information on impending new legislation, standards and best practice. They regularly up-date organisations which are on their mailing lists with free information. Various 'hot line' services are also provided by these government departments. A wide range of information on food safety law and practice is available through HMSO.

Local government

LACOTS and local environmental health departments provide a range of information on food safety.

Liaison groups for lawyers

The Food Law Group offers to its member solicitors regular information. It can be contacted through the Law Society, 113 Chancery Lane, London WC2A 1PL.

Professional institutions

A number of professional institutions, including the Chartered Institute of Environmental Health, the Royal Society of Health, the Royal Institute of Public Health and Hygiene and LACOTS publish a wide range of material on food safety issues.

Appendix 1

FSA 1990 Codes of Practice

Food Safety Act 1990 Codes of Practice

1 Responsibility for enforcement of the Food Safety Act 1990
2 Legal matters
3 Inspection procedures – general
4 Inspection, detention and seizure of suspect food
5 The use of improvement notices (Revised April 1994)
6 Prohibition procedures
7 Sampling for analysis or examination
8 Food standards inspections
9 Food hygiene inspections (Revised September 1995)
10 Enforcement of temperature control requirements of food hygiene regulations.
11 Enforcement of the Food Premises (Registration) Regulations
12 Division of enforcement responsibilities for the Quick Frozen Foodstuffs Regulations 1990
13 Enforcement of the Food Safety Act 1990 in relation to Crown Premises
14 Enforcement of the Food Safety (Live Bivalve Molluscs and Other Shellfish) Regulations 1992
15 Enforcement of the Food Safety (Fishery Products) Regulations 1992 and associated regulations
16 Enforcement of the Food Safety Act 1990 in relation to the food hazard warning system
17 Enforcement of the Meat Products (Hygiene) Regulations 1994
18 Enforcement of the Dairy Products (Hygiene) Regulations 1995 and the Dairy Products (Hygiene) (Scotland) Regulations 1995

Appendix 2

Prescribed Forms

Detention of Food (Prescribed Forms) Regulations 1990 (SI 1990 No 2614)

Form 1

Authority: . . . .

Food Safety Act 1990 – Section 9
DETENTION OF FOOD NOTICE

Reference Number:
1. To: . . . .
   Of: . . . .
   . . . .

2. Food to which this notice applies:
   Description : . . . .
   Quantity : . . . .
   Identification marks : . . . .

3. *THIS FOOD IS NOT TO BE USED FOR HUMAN CONSUMPTION.*
   In my opinion, the food does not comply with food safety requirements because: . . . .
   . . . .
   . . . .

178

4. The food must not be removed from:

    . . . .

    . . . .

    *unless it is moved to:

    . . . .

    . . . .

    (*Officer to delete if not applicable)

5. Within 21 days, either this notice will be withdrawn and the food
    released, or the food will be seized to be dealt with by a justice of the
    peace, or in Scotland a sheriff or magistrate, who may condemn it.

    Signed: . . . . Authorised Officer
    Name in capitals: . . . .
    Date: . . . .
    Address: . . . .
    . . . .
    . . . .
    Tel: . . . . Fax: . . . .

    > *Please read the notes overleaf care-*
    > *fully. If you are not sure of your rights*
    > *or the implications of this notice, you*
    > *may want to seek legal advice.*

NOTES

1. The food described in this notice has been detained pending official investigation.
2. The food must not be used for human consumption until it is released by the officer.
3. The food must remain where it is. If it is moved, it may only be moved to the place stated in paragraph 4 of the notice.
4. If for some reason you need to move the food after receiving this notice, you should contact the officer.
5. Within 21 days the officer must tell you if the notice is being withdrawn or if he is seizing the food for it to be dealt with by a justice of the peace, or in Scotland a sheriff or magistrate, who may condemn it.
6. *COMPENSATION:* If this notice is withdrawn and the food released for human consumption, then you may be entitled to compensation from the authority. This compensation will be payable for any loss in value of the food resulting from the effect of the notice.

WARNING

*FAILURE TO COMPLY KNOWINGLY WITH THIS
NOTICE IS AN OFFENCE*

Offenders will be liable:
*— on summary conviction, to a fine of up to £2000 and/or
6 months in prison,*
or
*— on conviction on indictment, to an unlimited fine and/or
up to 2 years in prison.*

Form 2

Authority: . . . .

Food Safety Act 1990 – Section 9
WITHDRAWAL OF DETENTION OF FOOD NOTICE

1. To: . . . .
   Of: . . . .
   . . . .

2. Detention Notice Number . . . ., dated . . . . and served
   on you on . . . . (date) is now withdrawn. The food described
   in paragraph 3 below can now be used for human consumption.

3. Food released for human consumption:
   Description   : . . . .
   Quantity   : . . . .
   Identification marks : . . . .

   Signed: . . . . Authorised Officer
   Name in capitals: . . . .
   Date: . . . .
   Address: . . . .
   . . . .
   . . . .
   Tel: . . . . Fax: . . . .

> *Please read the notes overleaf care-*
> *fully. If you are not sure of your rights*
> *or the implications of this notice, you*
> *may want to seek legal advice.*

NOTES

1. The food described in this notice has now been released for human consumption.
2. If this notice does not relate to all of the food originally detained, then the rest has been seized under section 9(3)(b) of the Food Safety Act 1990.
3. *COMPENSATION:* If you can show that any of the food now released for human consumption has lost value, you may be entitled to compensation from the authority. Compensation will be payable for any loss in value resulting from the effect of the notice.

Form 3

Authority: ....

Food Safety Act 1990 – Section 9
FOOD CONDEMNATION WARNING NOTICE

Reference Number:

1. To: ....
   Of: ....

2. This Notice applies to the following food which has been seized by an officer of this authority:
   Description   : ....
   Quantity   : ....
   Identification marks   : ....

3. *IT IS MY INTENTION TO APPLY TO A JUSTICE OF THE PEACE, OR IN SCOTLAND A SHERIFF OR MAGISTRATE, AT*
   ....
   ON ....*(DATE) AT* ...... *AM/PM FOR THE ABOVE FOOD TO BE CONDEMNED,*
   because ....

4. As the person in charge of the food, you are entitled to attend and to bring witnesses.

5. A copy of this notice has also been given to:
   ....
   ....
   who may also attend and bring witnesses.

   Signed: .... Authorised Officer
   Name in capitals: ....
   Date: ....
   Address: ....
   ....
   ....
   Tel: .... Fax: ....

> *Please read the notes overleaf carefully. If you are not sure of your rights or the implications of this notice, you may want to seek legal advice.*

NOTES

1. You are being warned that the Authority will be applying to a justice of the peace, or in Scotland a sheriff or magistrate, for the food that has already been seized to be condemned.
2. The justice of the peace, or in Scotland the sheriff or magistrate, will listen to the authority's case that the food fails to comply with food safety requirements and should be condemned. You may say why it should not be condemned.
3. You may bring your own evidence and witnesses to challenge the views of the authority and you may be represented by a lawyer.
4. You are not being charged with an offence. The hearing is only to decide whether the food complies with food safety requirements. But the court may order the food to be condemned. However you may be prosecuted for offences under the Food Safety Act 1990.
5. *EXPENSES:* If the justice of the peace, or in Scotland the sheriff or magistrate, orders the food to be condemned, then the owner of the food will have to pay reasonable expenses for it to be destroyed or disposed of.
6. *COMPENSATION:* If the justice of the peace, or in Scotland the sheriff or magistrate, does not condemn the food, the owner of the food may be entitled to compensation from the authority for any loss in its value as a result of the action taken by the authority.

Food Safety (Improvement and Prohibition – Prescribed Forms) Regulations 1991 (SI 1991 No 100)

Form 1

Authority: ....

Food Safety Act 1990 – Section 10
IMPROVEMENT NOTICE

Reference Number:

1. To: .... (Proprietor of the food business)
   At: ....
   ....
   .... (Address of proprietor)

2. In my opinion the:
   ....
   ....
   [Officer to insert matters which do not comply with the Regulations]
   in connection with your food business ....
   .... (Name of business)
   at ....
   .... (Address of business)
   do/does* not meet the requirements of ....
   of the .... Regulations
   because:
   ....
   ....
   [*Officer to delete as appropriate]

3. In my opinion, the following measures are needed for you to comply
   with these Regulations: ....
   ....
   ....

4. These measures or measures that will achieve the same effect must be
   taken by: .... (date)

5. *It is an offence not to comply with this improvement notice by the date
   stated.*

   Signed: .... Authorised Officer
   Name in capitals: ....

Date: . . . .

Address: . . . .

. . . .

Tel: . . . .   Fax: . . . .

> *Please read the notes overleaf care-*
> *fully. If you are not sure of your rights*
> *or the implications of this notice, you*
> *may want to seek legal advice.*

NOTES

1. In the opinion of the officer you are not complying with the Regulations under Part II of the Food Safety Act 1990 described in paragraph 2 of the notice. The work needed in the officer's opinion to put matters right is described and it must be finished by the date set.
2. You are responsible for ensuring that the work is carried out within the period specified, which must be at least 14 days.
3. *You have a right to carry out work that will achieve the same effect as that described in the notice.* If you think that there is another equally effective way of complying with the law, you should first discuss it with the officer.

YOUR RIGHT OF APPEAL

4. If you disagree with all or part of this notice, you can appeal to the magistrates' court, or in Scotland to the sheriff. You must appeal within one calendar month of the date of the notice or the period ending with the date stated in paragraph 4 of the notice, whichever ends earlier.
5. If you decide to appeal, the time set out in the notice is suspended and you do not have to carry out the work described until the appeal is heard. *However, if you are not complying with the Regulations mentioned in the notice, you may still be prosecuted for failure to comply with those Regulations.*
6. When the appeal is heard, the magistrates' court, or in Scotland the sheriff, may confirm, cancel or vary the notice.

WARNING

FAILURE TO COMPLY WITH THIS NOTICE IS AN OFFENCE

*Offenders are liable to be fined and/or
imprisoned for up to 2 years.*

Form 2

Authority: . . . .

Food Safety Act 1990 – Section 12
EMERGENCY PROHIBITION NOTICE

Reference Number:

1. To: . . . . (Proprietor of the food business)

    At: . . . .

    . . . .

    . . . . (Address of proprietor)

2* I am satisfied that: . . . .

    . . . .

    . . . .

    at . . . .

    . . . . (Address of business)

POSES AN IMMINENT RISK OF INJURY TO HEALTH because:

    . . . .

    . . . .

    . . . .

(*See Note 1 overleaf)

3. *YOU MUST NOT USE IT FOR THE PURPOSES OF THIS/ANY/*
    THIS OR ANY SIMILAR* FOOD BUSINESS.
    [*Officer to delete as appropriate]

    Signed: . . . . Authorised Officer

    Name in capitals: . . . .

    Date: . . . .

    Address: . . . .

    . . . .

    Tel: . . . . Fax: . . . .

> *Please read the notes overleaf care-*
> *fully. If you are not sure of your rights*
> *or the implications of this notice, you*
> *may want to seek legal advice.*

NOTES

1. *When you receive this notice you must IMMEDIATELY stop using the premises, process, treatment or equipment described by the officer in paragraph 2 of the notice and located at the address stated.*
2. Within 3 days of service of this notice, the authority must apply to a magistrates' court, or in Scotland to a sheriff, for an order confirming the prohibition. You will be told the date of the hearing which you are entitled to attend and at which you may call witnesses if you wish.
3. If you believe that you have acted to remove the imminent risk of injury to health, you should apply in writing to the authority for a certificate which would allow you to use the premises, process, treatment or equipment again. You can do this even if the court hearing has not taken place.
4. You are not allowed to use the premises, process, treatment or equipment for the purpose specified in paragraph 3 of the notice (see section 11(3) of the Food Safety Act 1990) until (a) a court decides you may do so; (b) the authority issues you with a certificate as in paragraph 3 above; (c) 3 days have passed since the service of the notice and the authority has not applied to the court as in paragraph 2 above; or (d) the authority abandons the application.
5. A copy of this notice must, by law, be fixed on the premises or equipment which is not to be used. It is an offence (under section 1 of the Criminal Damage Act 1971 or, in Scotland, section 78 of the Criminal Justice (Scotland) Act 1980) to deface it.
6. *COMPENSATION:* If the authority does not apply to the magistrates' court, or in Scotland to the sheriff, for an order confirming its action within 3 days of the date of service of this notice, you will be entitled to compensation for any losses you have suffered because you could not use the premises, process, treatment or equipment because you were complying with this notice. You will also be entitled to such compensation if the magistrates' court, or in Scotland the sheriff, decide at the hearing that the authority's action was wrong.

WARNING

ANYONE WHO KNOWINGLY CONTRAVENES THIS NOTICE IS GUILTY OF AN OFFENCE

Offenders are liable to be fined and/or imprisoned for up to 2 years.

Form 3

Authority: . . . .

Food Safety Act 1990 – Section 12

NOTICE OF INTENTION TO APPLY FOR AN EMERGENCY PROHIBITION ORDER

Reference Number:

1. To: . . . .
    Address: . . . .
    . . . .
    . . . .

    You are the proprietor of the food business at:

    . . . .
    . . . .
    . . . .

2. *I give notice that I shall be applying to the* . . . .
    Magistrates' Court/Sheriff sitting at . . . .
    for an emergency prohibition order because . . . .
    . . . .
    . . . .

3. If an order is made by the court you will not be able to use the premises, process, treatment or equipment described:

    . . . .
    . . . .
    . . . .

    for the purpose of this/any or any similar* food business.
    [*Officer to delete as appropriate]

    Signed: . . . . Authorised Officer
    Name in capitals: . . . .
    Date: . . . .
    Address: . . . .
    . . . .
    Tel: . . . . Fax: . . . .

> *Please read the notes overleaf carefully. If you are not sure of your rights or the implications of this notice, you may want to seek legal advice.*

NOTES

1. This notice tells you that the authority intends to apply to the magistrates' court, or in Scotland the sheriff, for an emergency prohibition order which, if granted, would mean that you could not use the premises, process, treatment or equipment described for the purposes specified in paragraph 3 of the notice (see section 11(3) of the Food Safety Act 1990).

2. The court will consider the evidence from the authority as to why they believe there is an imminent risk of injury to health from the operation of your food business or part of it. You may bring your own evidence and witnesses to put before the court and you may choose to be represented by a lawyer.

3. *If the court is convinced by the authority's evidence, then an order will be made stating what you may not do. The order will be served on you by the authority. A copy of it must be fixed by the authority at your premises and it is an offence to deface it. (Section 1 of the Criminal Damage Act 1971 or, in Scotland, section 78 of the Criminal Justice (Scotland) Act 1980).*

4. In England and Wales, you have the right to appeal to the Crown Court against the decision of the magistrates' court if you think that it is wrong. In Scotland the position is governed by the Rules of Court.

5. The making of an order does not mean you are guilty of an offence but the authority may seek to prosecute you for offences under the Food Safety Act 1990 or associated regulations.

6. If you have been issued with an emergency prohibition notice from the authority, you will know what steps should be taken to remove the imminent risk to health.

7. *If the court is not satisfied by the authority's evidence and an order is not issued, then you will be entitled to continue your business. If the authority has already issued you with an emergency prohibition notice and you have suffered loss because you have complied with it, then you will also be entitled to compensation from the authority.*

Form 4

Authority: . . . .

Food Safety Act 1990 – Sections 11 & 12

CERTIFICATE THAT THERE IS NO LONGER A RISK TO HEALTH

1. To: . . . . (Name of proprietor)
    At: . . . . (Address of proprietor)
    Proprietor of: . . . .
    Address of food business: . . . .
    . . . .

2. *The enforcement authority certifies that it is satisfied that you have taken sufficient measures to secure the removal of the imminent* risk of injury to health described in the*:

    > emergency prohibition notice*
    > emergency prohibition order*
    > prohibition order*
    > [*Officer to delete as appropriate]

    served on you on . . . . (date).

    Signed:. . . . . Authorised Officer
    Name in capitals: . . . .
    Date: . . . .
    Address: . . . .
    . . . .
    Tel: . . . . Fax: . . . .

THIS CERTIFICATE MEANS THAT YOU MAY NOW USE THE PREMISES, PROCESS, TREATMENT OR EQUIPMENT AGAIN.

> *Please read the notes overleaf carefully. If you are not sure of your rights or the implications of this notice, you may want to seek legal advice.*

NOTES

1. The authority is now satisfied that the imminent* risk of injury to health no longer exists in respect of the circumstances that caused the authority to issue you with an emergency prohibition notice or the court to impose a prohibition order or emergency prohibition order.
2. *The relevant notice or order is now lifted and you may use the premises, process, treatment or equipment again.*
   [*Officer to delete as appropriate]

Form 5

Authority: . . . .

Food Safety Act 1990 – Sections 11 & 12
NOTICE OF CONTINUING RISK TO HEALTH

1. To: . . . . (Name of proprietor)
   At: . . . . (Address of proprietor)
   Proprietor of: . . . .
   Address of food business: . . . .
   . . . .

2. *The authority is NOT satisfied that you have taken sufficient measures to secure the removal of the imminent* risk of injury to health described in the*:

   emergency prohibition notice*
   emergency prohibition order*
   prohibition order*
   [*Officer to delete as appropriate]

   served on you on . . . . (date), a further copy of which is attached.
   The authority is not satisfied because: . . . .
   . . . .
   . . . .

3. *You must not use the premises, process, treatment or equipment in question until the authority notifies you that you may do so.*

   Signed: . . . . Authorised Officer
   Name in capitals: . . . .
   Date: . . . .
   Address: . . . .
   . . . .
   Tel: . . . . Fax: . . . .

   > *Please read the notes overleaf care-*
   > *fully. If you are not sure of your rights*
   > *or the implications of this notice, you*
   > *may want to seek legal advice.*

NOTES

1. The authority is not yet satisfied that the imminent* risk of injury to health has been removed at your business. The reasons why the authority is not satisfied are given.
2. You still cannot use the premises, process, treatment or equipment in question for the purposes described in the emergency prohibition notice/emergency prohibition order/prohibition order* even if you are appealing against the terms of this notice.
3. You are entitled to appeal against this notice. If you want to do so, you should apply to the magistrates' court, or in Scotland to a sheriff, within one calendar month of the date on which this notice is served on you.
4. As soon as you think that there is no longer a/an imminent* risk of injury to health, because of actions you have taken, you may apply to the authority for the prohibition notice or order to be lifted.
   [*Officer to delete as appropriate]

WARNING

FAILURE TO COMPLY WITH THE ORIGINAL NOTICE
OR ORDER IS AN OFFENCE

Offenders are liable to be fined and/or imprisoned for
up to 2 years.

The Food Safety (Sampling and Qualifications) Regulations 1990 (SI 1990 No 2463)

Schedule 3

Regulation 9(2)

Certificate of Analysis or Examination carried out under Food Safety (Sampling and Qualifications) Regulations 1990

To:
(name and address of person who originally submitted the sample)

I, the undersigned
* public analyst for
* food analyst
* food examiner

certify that at (time) _____   on the (date)   Day Month Year ____ 1 9
the sample marked:

Date sample taken	Reference number, description etc.	Weight or measure This column may be left blank if the sample could not be conveniently weighed or measured or the weight or measurement is not material to the result

was received by me:
* from you (the person named above)

OR * from
(insert the name and address of the analyst / examiner to whom the sample was first submitted)

I certify that the sample was *analysed/examined by me, or under my direction and the results are as follows:

If necessary please continue overleaf

My opinion and observations are:
(if deemed appropriate by analyst/examiner

If necessary please continue overleaf

I further certify that the sample had undergone no change which would affect my results, opinion or observations.

(This statement is required if the sample has been analysed. It should be deleted if the certificate relates to food examination)

Certified by me this _____ day of _____ at (place) _____

Signature _____   Status _____

Name in BLOCK LETTERS _____

Official address _____

Telephone No. _____

---

*Delete as appropriate

Appendix 3

Principal Labelling Information Required by Statute

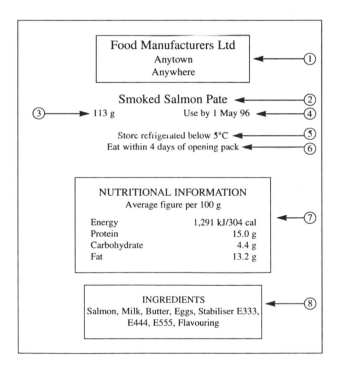

Food Manufacturers Ltd
Anytown
Anywhere — ①

Smoked Salmon Pate ◄— ②
③ —► 113 g   Use by 1 May 96 ◄— ④

Store refrigerated below 5°C ◄— ⑤
Eat within 4 days of opening pack ◄— ⑥

NUTRITIONAL INFORMATION
Average figure per 100 g

Energy	1,291 kJ/304 cal
Protein	15.0 g
Carbohydrate	4.4 g
Fat	13.2 g

◄— ⑦

INGREDIENTS
Salmon, Milk, Butter, Eggs, Stabiliser E333,
E444, E555, Flavouring

◄— ⑧

Notes

① Name and address of manufacturer, packer or seller in the EU (see reg 6(e) of the Food Labelling Regulations 1984).
② Name of food (see regs 6(a) and 7–10 and Sched 1 of the Food Labelling Regulations 1984).

③   Weight (see s 48 of the Weights and Measures Act 1985).
④   Durability indication – use-by or best-before date (see regs 6(c), 21, 21(a) and 22 of the Food Labelling Regulations 1984).
⑤   Special storage conditions (see reg 6(d) of the Food Labelling Regulations 1984).
⑥   Special conditions of use (see regs 6(d) and 23 of the Food Labelling Regulations 1984).
⑦   Nutritional information (see regs 36 and 37 and Sched 6A of the Food Labelling Regulations 1984).
⑧   Ingredients (see regs 6(b) and 13–20 of the Food Labelling Regulations 1984).

See Chapter 3, pp 36–7 for further discussion of labelling requirements.

Index

Contamination of food—*contd*
  causes, 27–8
  clostridium botulinum, by, 29
  decomposition of food, 30
  examples, 27–8
  hand, by, 29–30
  manner of, 27–8
  nature of, 27
  poisoning caused by, 29
  sources, 27–8
  spoilage of food, 30
  toxins caused by, 29
Contractors, 172
Crown Court appeals—
  from, 19
  to, 17–18
Crown premises, 8

Decomposition of food, 30
Defences—
  advertiser's, 92
  amendment of summons, 76
  another person's fault, 78–9
  branded goods sellers, 82–4
  constituent elements not proved, 78
  defendant's identity, 76
  delay in prosecution, 73–4
  due diligence, *see* Due diligence
    defence
  duplicity, 74–5
  fault of another person, 78–9
  generally, 72
  importer of food, 81–2
  multiple offences charged, 74–5
  notice requirements, 89–90
  own labeller, 82
  person summoned, identity of, 76
  preparer of food, 81–2
  procedural matters, 72
  prosecutor's identity, 77
  substantive, 77 *et seq*
  time limits, 72–4
  see also Offences
Descriptions of food—
  false, 34, 35
  misleading, 34
  'natural' products, 35
  traditional, 36
Destruction of food, 125, 126
Detention of food—
  batches of food, 125–6
  Code of Practice, 121
  consignments of food, 125–6

Detention of food—*contd*
  contravention of notice, 121
  expenses, 125
  inspection, after, 121
  lots, food in, 125–6
  magistrate's role, 124–5
  notice, 121–2, 123, 178–80
  seizure compared, 121
  withdrawal of notice, 122, 181–2
Development of law, 1–3
Disease notification, 45–6
Disposal of food, 125
Distribution chain, 154–5
Distributors, 155
Doors, 53
Drainage facilities, 52
Due diligence defence—
  advising client, 156–8
  basis, 80–1
  branded goods seller, 82–4, 173
  burden of proof, 80–1
  causal link, 81
  checks, 90–1
  cleaning schedules, 90
  Codes of Practice, 80–1, 88–9
  consumer complaints, 91
  corrective action, 91
  deemed, 82–4, 173
  delegation of functions, 85–6
  director's liability, 85
  documented procedures, 88
  enforcement, procedures following, 91
  factors affecting, 86
  guidance on standards, 87
  hazard analysis, 89
  importer of food, 81–2
  infestation control arrangements, 90
  inspections, 88–9
  liaison with food authority officers, 91
  management systems, 89–92
  meaning of due diligence, 85–8
  mission statements, 89–90
  notice requirements, 84–5
  offences, applicable, 80
  own labellers, 82
  planned preventative maintenance, 90
  policy statements, 89–90
  precautions, 91
  preparer of food, 81–2
  proving, 88–9

Food—
  application of Act, 8–9
  contact materials, 7
  definition, 6
  exclusions, 6
  handlers, *see* Handlers of food
  premises, 7
  sale of, 6–7
  sources, 7
Food Advisory Committee, 103
Food business regulation—
  advertising for sale, 9, 11
  ambit of, 10
  application of statutory provisions,
    8–9
  'business', 8
  commercial operation, 8, 9
  Crown premises, 8
  enforcement authorities, *see*
    Enforcement
  entertainments, public, 9
  exposing for sale, 9, 10
  food, definition of, 6–7
  human consumption—
    'not for sale for', 11, 12
    presumption of intention, 11–12
  intention to sell food, 10
  offering for sale, 9
  possessing for sale, 9, 10–11
  premises, 7
  proprietor, 8
  sale of food, 9
  sources, food, 7
  'supply of food otherwise than by
    sale', 9–10
  unseen products, 10
Food hazard warning system, 149
Food poisoning, *see* Contamination of
  food
Food safety—
  Act of 1990, 6 *et seq*
  offences, *see* Offences
  requirements, *see* Food safety
    requirements
Food safety requirements—
  definition, 25
  offence of non-compliance—
    batches of food, 26
    contamination, *see* Contamina-
      tion of food
    effect, 27–30
    evidential issues, 27–8

Food safety requirements   *contd*
  general product safety regulations
    and, 26–7
  implications, 27–30
  in-factory enforcement, 24
  meaning, 25
  prosecutions, 24
  statutory basis, 24
  unfitness for human consump-
    tion, 25–6
  unwholesomeness, 24–5
Formal caution procedure, 21–2

Genetically modified food sources, 95–6

HACCP—
  see Hazard analysis critical control
    points system
Handlers of food—
  disease notification, 45–6
  meaning, 60
  supervision, 90–1
  training, 60–1, 90–1
Hazard analysis critical control points
  system (HACCP)—
  advantages, 159 60
  basic principles, 158
  biological hazards, 158
  chemical hazards, 158
  control point, 158–9
  critical control points, 159
  disease causing hazards, 158
  hazard defined, 158
  implementation, 160
  meaning, 45, 89
  monitoring procedures, 160
  review of system, 160–1
  stages, 159
Health surveillance, 167–8
High Court—
  appeals to, 18–19
  case stated procedure, 18–19
Historical background, 1–3
Hygiene of food—
  'adequate', 48
  'appropriate' practices, 48, 49
  assured safe catering (ASC), 45, 161
  ceilings, 53
  changing facilities, 52
  clean person strategies, 49, 58
  clean place strategies, 49
  construction of premises, 50